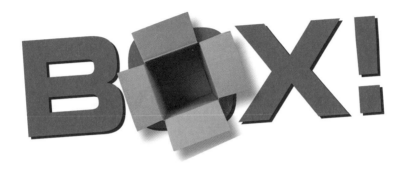

Also by Noel MacNeal

10-Minute Puppets

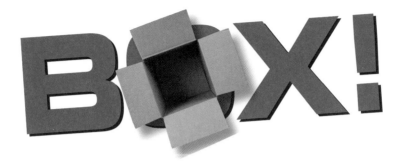

BOX!

Castles, Kitchens, and Other
Cardboard Creations for Kids

Noel MacNeal

LYONS PRESS
Guilford, Connecticut
An imprint of Globe Pequot Press

To buy books in quantity for corporate use
or incentives, call **(800) 962-0973**
or e-mail **premiums@GlobePequot.com.**

Lyons Press is an imprint of Globe Pequot Press.

Project editor: Ellen Urban
Design and layout: Sue Murray

Library of Congress Cataloging-in-Publication Data

MacNeal, Noel.
Box! : castles, kitchens, and other cardboard creations for kids / Noel MacNeal.
pages cm
Summary: "How many times have you spent money on some fancy new toy for your child, only to have her ignore the toy and instead crawl into the large box it came in? Whether you're on a budget or just refuse to pay high prices for noisy, plastic toys, *Box!* offers parents do-it-yourself, environmentally friendly crafts that can be made with cereal boxes, packing boxes, toilet paper rolls, and egg cartons. Filled with easy to make cardboard box craft ideas complete with supply lists, four-color photos, tips, and templates, *Box!* supplies parents with projects that will keep their children entertained for hours, such as: making "little people" with toilet paper rolls; creating a pirate ship out of a milk carton; fashioning a telescope using a paper towel tube; assembling planes, trains, and automobiles from cracker boxes, pasta boxes, or toothpaste boxes; and even constructing a child-sized desk out of three large boxes. This book is the perfect way to make fun, inexpensive, sustainable toys for your little one"— Provided by publisher.
ISBN 978-0-7627-8777-7 (paperback)
1. Box craft. 2. Paperboard. 3. Handicraft for children. I. Title.
TT870.5.M33 2013
745.54—dc23
2013030982

Printed in the United States of America

10 9 8 7 6 5 4 3 2 1

*To Matthew Wallace MacNeal, whose imagination helps mine
go places I've never been before.*

Thanks, Mattie.

CONTENTS

FOREWORD
My Life as a Box So Far

by A. Box

So far I've been a shopping bag, a turtle, almost a cradle, and a TV set. Of course, I started out as a box. A box that carried cans of sauce. Twenty-four cans of Del Monte Tomato Sauce, all in straight rows, one on top of the other, from the bottom of me all the way to my top.

I became a delivery box when a grocer needed something in which to carry his next order. He filled me up with a bag of rice, a can of beans, a box of spaghetti, and quarts of milk and delivered me to a little girl's house. Soon after her mother took the food out of me and I was empty, the little girl put me on her back and started to crawl around like she was a turtle!

After a few days of that she tried to turn me into a cradle for her baby doll by stuffing me with a pillow and laying her doll on top. I couldn't rock very well because of my flat bottom, so when she got tired of clunking me from side to side, she settled for making believe I was a bed.

Next, her cousin came over, made a hole in my side, stuck his head in, and started singing "O Sole Mio" at the top of his lungs like he was a singer on TV. Who would've thought—me, a television star—I mean, a television set!

Just goes to show all the things you can be in life. With this book that Noel MacNeal wrote, I wonder what I'll be next . . . A rocket ship? A gas station?

What about you? What are some of the things you're going to think of?

—As told to Sonia Manzano (an author and "Maria" from the Daytime Emmy Award–winning children's series, *Sesame Street*)

P.S. When I was a kid, groceries were carried home in boxes. My brothers and I often had fun using the boxes for all sorts of things, until they fell apart! I hope you have fun with Noel's book, and boxes, too!
—Sonia Manzano

INTRODUCTION: OUT OF THE BOX

I'm a dad of a (currently) very imaginative eight-year-old (going on forty-two).

I'm also a professional *puppeteer.* That's right; you read it correctly. Puppeteer. I've worked on TV shows and commercials, in movies, and onstage for thirty years. I'm proud to say that my résumé now is many people's childhood memories.

These two fields of expertise helped me create my first book, *10-Minute Puppets.* It was my wife's idea. She said, "You know how to be a dad, and you know how to be a puppeteer. Why not combine these experiences in a book to show families how easy and fun puppet-making can be?" (She also said, "But don't make it 'crafty.' Make it for people like me. You are not married to Martha Stewart.") So that's what I did, because they were not only characters I created with and for my son, but also ones I remember building when I was a kid.

But of course, as a parent, I know that kids like to play with more than one type of toy, so I haven't just been making puppets for the past seven years. Oh, far from it.

The inspiration for this book came from an experience with my son when he was a toddler. Our local, indoor play area had one of those kitchens kids can pretend to "cook" and "bake" with, so naturally, I thought we should get one for him. Then I went online and saw the prices. My knee-jerk reaction was "You want HOW MUCH for THIS?!" Most parents start buying stuff even before their kids are born, and it only continues as the years go by. But when I saw this, my next natural reaction was, "I could make one!" This kitchen was the first thing I made out of boxes for him, and I haven't stopped.

BOX! will help you to create all kinds of things with your kids—not just out of boxes, but out of any container that comes your way via the grocery store, mail, or special delivery. Take-out, tissue, cereal, and cracker boxes—even cardboard paper-towel and bathroom-tissue tubes—will all be fair game for creativity.

Kids are great at "instant play." You know what I mean: Flip that big box your new *fill-in-the-blank* came in, and they have a rocket. Or a cave. Or a car. You don't need to do a thing except maybe join in (which I highly recommend; when was the last time your car drove to the moon?). So the majority of these projects fall under "instant play." Minimal crafting for you and the kids, followed by fun; this is because kids already have an active imagination, and they don't really care how it looks. They already know how it looks in their mind's eye! And as a parent, I already have a busy schedule. So "simple, quick, and easy" are the words that form the philosophy of this book.

Plus, you get to reuse, recycle, and even "upcycle" those boxes that come into your home. Good for you, good for the planet: win-win. In fact, I encourage you to reuse any of these boxes for other box projects. Get creative and combine them. Have you ever wanted a rocket ship or a fire truck? You can have both! I will help with step-by-step instructions, as well as some templates in the back of this book that you just need to color, cut out, and glue on. And when you have more time, or when everyone wants to create together, there are sidebars entitled "You Can Also Do This" to add highlights and details to any of these projects.

That said, there are a few things you will need (and it's likely you already have some of them on hand).

WHAT YOU WILL NEED

Materials

Well, you have at least one of the main components needed for a book entitled *BOX!*: a box, whether it comes from a store or through the mail. And you can easily boxes for free! The US Post Office has free shipping boxes, and supermarkets and appliance stores have boxes they don't need once the supplies are in. Just ask if you can have one (or a few). Here are some other things you'll need, which are most likely already in your kitchen junk drawer:

- Scissors
- Pencils
- Crayons/markers
- Glue (either stick or good old-fashioned "school" glue)

See? We're off to a great start already!

You might have a ruler for measuring off certain projects, but if not, no worries. Just use your index finger. An adult index finger from tip to knuckle is just over 3 inches, so you always have a ruler "on hand." (Sorry; couldn't resist.)

When you need to cut out certain shapes, such as a circle or square or rectangle, ballpark it. Just do it. It won't ruin anything; in fact, it will just make it more unique. But you can also, depending on the size needed, trace around a cup or plate for circles, or a book or postcard for rectangles.

Now, there are a few things you may need to buy if you don't have them already.

• Duct Tape

This will be your friend. Get a big roll, and it will last you well beyond these projects. It's indispensable for "instant play."

• Hot Glue Gun and Sticks

This is very important: A hot glue gun is a fantastic tool for these crafts, but it is a tool. There's a reason why it has the word *hot* in it. As a responsible author (and parent), I do need to say that you should NEVER, EVER leave an unattended hot glue gun with a child in the room. (There. Moving on.)

• Velcro

This can be obtained not only at hardware stores, but also at most major drugstore chains. I love Velcro. It can be an instant "lock" or "latch" to keep the pirate chest or magic book closed.

• Box Cutter

This is a great tool for cutting thick cardboard. It goes without saying that ONLY AN ADULT should use this tool. Be careful when cutting; there's no need to rush. And NEVER leave a box cutter unattended with a child around.

• Scrap Cardboard

This is some of the leftover cardboard you'll have from one project that can be applied to other projects. Even postcards you get in the mail or the "blow-ins" (as they're called) that get placed in magazines qualify as scrap cardboard.

Also, if you have a home office, you'll use your printer and paper. Why? Because once you've used up the templates in the back of this book, you can just go to my website (noelmacneal.com) to download and print more pages.

CHAPTER ONE

Little Boxes and Containers

I feel we get more of these types of boxes than any other, bringing most of them into our homes from the grocery store. Cereal, snack, and frozen-food boxes—even milk cartons and the cardboard tubes in rolls of paper towels and bathroom tissue—they all have such playful potential once their contents are emptied. And they are perfect for creating, well . . . these!

Herb Garden

It's true; there is nothing like fresh herbs to add zest to your meals. And growing your own not only gives you a sense of pride, but also teaches the kids in your life how easy healthy living can be—and how delicious it can taste!

Materials:

- A milk carton
- Scissors
- Potting soil
- Seeds
- Water
- Construction paper or gift wrap (optional)

Directions

1. Wash and dry the milk carton. Then use the scissors to . . .

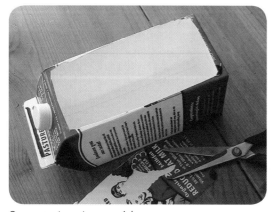

2. . . . cut out one side.

3. Fill the carton with the soil.

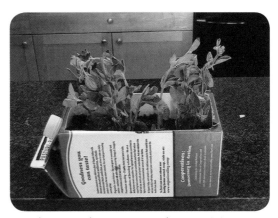

4. Using your finger or a pencil, make little trenches in the soil. Plant the seeds and water them.

5. When ready, reap your harvest!

You Can Also Do This

This also makes a sweet flower box. Wrap construction paper (or gift wrap) around the milk carton and plant any flowers you wish.

Little People

I've been a puppeteer ever since I was a kid, and so have you. It's true. Ever made your favorite doll or stuffed animal or action figure walk, talk, or sneak up behind Mom and say "BOO!"? That's puppeteering. And these puppets are easy to make. By using the templates for these folks, you'll make new friends in no time flat. Literally! Then they can move into their brand-new home (see Dollhouse, on page 59), or put on a show with the Puppet Stage (see page 98).

Materials

- Scissors
- Little People templates (pages 143–45)
- Crayons/markers
- Bathroom-tissue tube
- Tape
- Glitter glue (optional)

Directions

1. Cut out the template and color it in.

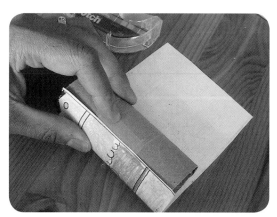

2. Tape the end of the template to one side of the tube and wrap the rest of it around.

3. Tape down the other side.

4. Now, let's play!

You Can Also Do This

Use glitter glue to decorate and highlight your little person's features—their clothes, their hats, even their lips. Woo-hoo!

Mask #1: Masquerade

This is a classic cardboard craft from my childhood. Some cereal boxes used to have the masks on the back to cut out and wear, but when they didn't, I created my own. And now you can, too!

This is based on one style of masquerade: masks attached to a stick and held up to one's face.

Materials

- Copy or construction paper
- Crayons/markers
- Scissors
- Cereal box
- Glue
- Chopstick or drinking straw
- Tape
- Feathers, sequins, glitter, fabric (optional)

Directions

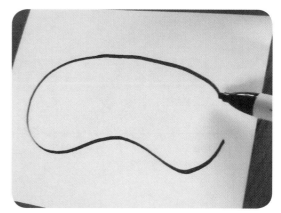

1. Draw a mask on paper.

2. Cut open the cereal box and lay it flat on a table.

3. Then glue the mask to one side.

4. Color and cut out the mask. (An adult should cut out the eyeholes.)

5. Flip the mask over and tape the straw or chopstick to one side of the mask.

6. Now hold it up to your face.
BOO!

You Can Also Do This

The masks used for masquerades come from Italy—specifically, the celebration of Carnival in Venice. Masks can be adorned with feathers, sequins, glitter, and fabric. You can also choose to use string or a long rubber band to attach to the mask (rather than the straw/chopstick option), to keep your hands free.

My Bank

Those baby-wipe dispensers have to be good for something else, right? You did spend good money on them, so why not use them to *save* money? Every kid needs a piggy bank to learn about the importance of saving. This project already teaches one good lesson: You don't need to spend money to have your own bank. Plus, it already has that natural slot for coins (and the holiday/birthday bill from my son's "Grandmama").

Materials

- Baby-wipe dispenser
- Construction paper
- Crayons/markers
- Scissors
- Glue

Directions

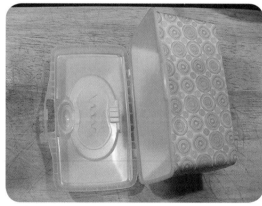

1. Clean and dry the interior of the dispenser.

2. Draw money symbols on the construction paper and cut them out. Then draw a "bank entrance" (a door with a sign above it that says bank).

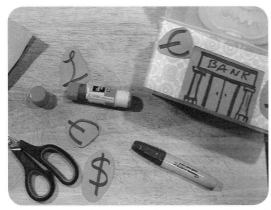

3. Glue your designs to the sides and top of the dispenser.

4. Then, gather your coins and start saving!

You Can Also Do This

Wrap construction paper around the sides and draw a "strongbox," with a lock in front and bolts on the side.

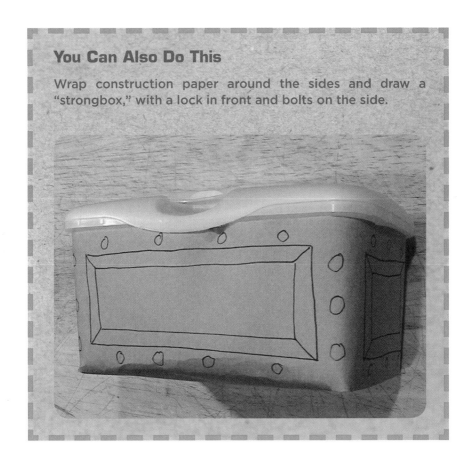

Pantry Wares

This is one of the simplest and quickest crafts in this book. All you are doing is collecting empty food boxes to be used in your soon-to-be-built Kitchen (see page 129). After all, everyone needs a well-stocked pantry for all those pretend snacks and make-believe banquets.

Materials

- Cereal boxes (especially those mini ones)
- Frozen-food boxes
- Cracker boxes
- Milk cartons
- Juice cartons
- Paper plates
- Plastic utensils
- Plastic jars and bottles

Directions

1. Clean out the boxes and cartons and tape them closed to reinforce them. Wash out plastic containers. Let them dry.

You Can Also Do This

We all have favorite brands we routinely buy; now you can make up your own! Create your own labels (by just drawing them on paper and cutting them out, or printing them out from your computer) and attach them to the empty boxes and containers.

Picture Frame

A picture is worth a thousand words, and any picture from my son is always given a place of honor on my desk or front door. Kids feel proud when they see their artwork displayed, and how cool, to have it framed for all the world to see! Here's an easy, nonbreakable frame that you can decorate for any artistic masterpiece or photographic memento.

Materials

- Box (such as a cereal box or box a toy came in)
- Scissors
- Crayons/markers
- Ruler
- Glue
- Construction paper
- Glitter glue, stickers, etc. (optional)
- Magnetic strips (optional)

Directions

1. Cut open the box and lay it flat.

2. Lay the drawing or photo on it and trace around it twice with a marker or crayon so that you have two cardboard rectangles.

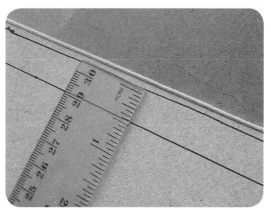

3. With a ruler, measure about half an inch from the outside line of the traced lines and draw another rectangle within.

4. Cut out the rectangle. (Note: An adult needs to cut out the inner rectangle.)

5. Put glue along the edge of the cut-out frame.

6. Lay the artwork or photo onto the glue side of the frame.

7. Add glue to the back of the artwork or photo.

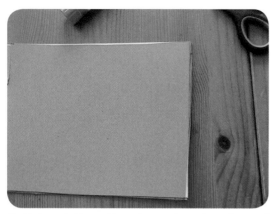

8. Cut out the other traced rectangle and lay it atop the glue.

9. Flip the frame over and decorate it with glitter glue, stickers, or whatever else you want.

10. Now, put it in a place of honor!

You Can Also Do This

Add magnetic strips from your local hardware, stationery, or craft store. Attach them to the back of your frame, and it's ready to hang on your fridge or any metal door.

Pirate Ship

Avast ye landlubbers, and take heed! You can create your own sailing vessel to sail the Spanish Main and seek out buried treasure, right in your own bathtub. But be warned: Once you cast off for adventure, there's no turning back!

Materials

- Milk carton
- Ruler
- Scissors
- Drinking straw or chopstick
- Tape
- Pirate Ship template (page 146)
- Crayons/markers
- Glue
- Construction paper, bathroom-tissue tube(s) (optional)

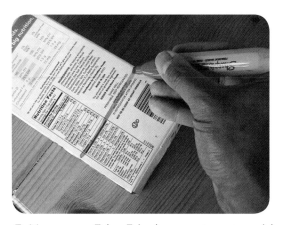

Directions

1. Wash out the milk carton and let it dry.

2. Turn the carton so that the front end has the "triangle" sides faceup and facedown.

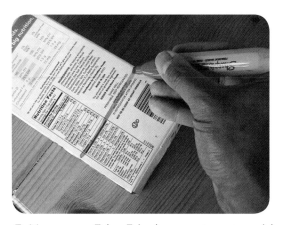

3. Measure a 3-by-3-inch square on one side of the carton. Cut it out.

4. Poke a hole about an inch in front of the square. Stick a straw or chopstick through the hole and tape the end onto the bottom of the carton.

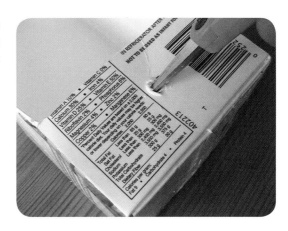

5. Cut out the sail and flag templates and poke the holes for the mast. Stick the chopstick through the holes.

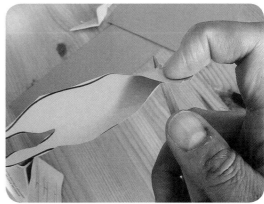

6. Color and cut out the portholes; then, glue them to the sides of the ship.

7. Cover the portholes with strips of tape to "waterproof" them.

8. Then, cast off in the bathtub!

You Can Also Do This

If you don't want to put your ship in water, you can wrap the carton with construction paper and draw your own design on it. You can also make a pirate based on the Little People template (page 145), and even a cannon for the deck. Just wrap black construction paper around a bathroom-tissue tube, cut out two circles, and glue them to the sides of the tube.

Ready? Aim? FIRE!

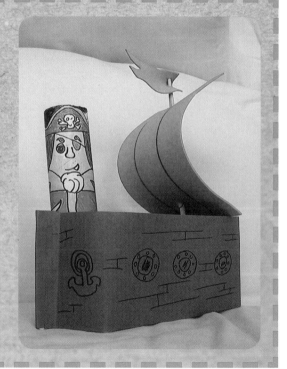

Puppets

My book *10-Minute Puppets* embraces the philosophy that anything can be a puppet, starting with one thing you have with you all the time . . . (Take a moment to think about what it is. Okay. Time's up.) . . . Your hand! So it stands to reason that a box can also be a puppet. In *10-Minute Puppets* I show how to make one out of a big box. Here's how to make puppets out of little boxes.

Materials

- A small box (preferably rectangular)
- Crayons/markers
- Scissors
- Tape
- Construction paper
- Glue

Directions

1. Draw a line across the middle of the box on three of its sides.

2. Use scissors to cut along the line. Bend the box in half.

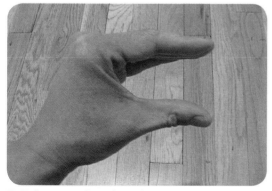

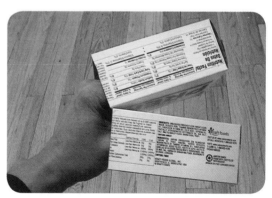

3. Take your hand and put your four fingers together and bend them down. Then tuck your thumb under. This is your "puppet hand." The box will slip onto your puppet hand.

4. To keep the box from slipping off your hand, make a strap. Just cut a 10-inch strip of construction paper.

5. Loop it around your four fingers and tape it closed. Add two strips of tape, sticky side facing down, slip it back onto your hand, and insert your hand in the box. Stick your strap to inside of box.

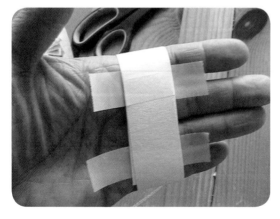

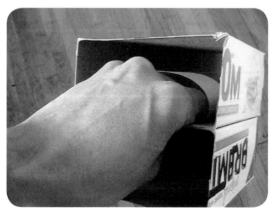

6. Draw eyes on a piece of construction paper, making sure the eyeballs are attached as one piece. Add dotted lines to the bottom. When you cut the eyes out, fold the paper along the dotted lines.

7. Glue the folded part of the eyes to the top of the box, near the back.

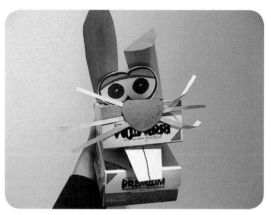

8. Ta-da! Puppet!

9. Now you can cut out and add any other features you'd like, to make any creature from your imagination.

You Can Also Do This

You can make a "person," or, in this case, a "monster." Color and decorate the box puppet with a face. Then draw and cut out a body and attach it to the bottom jaw. When you're ready, you can put on a show with your very own Puppet Stage (from chapter 3, page 98)!

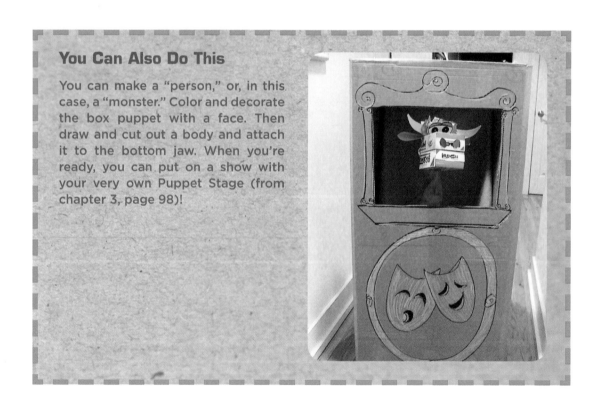

Planes, Trains, and Automobiles

All kids love vehicles, whether riding in them or just watching them go by. These simple toy versions can be adapted for most boxes (so even though I'll show you how to make the train, the basic steps apply for the others), and will have everyone ready to roll.

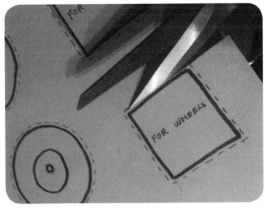

Materials

- Ride templates (pages 147–50)
- Crayons/markers
- Scissors
- Glue
- Box (a cracker box, pasta box, or toothpaste box)
- Cardboard (from a postcard, greeting card, or lightweight food box)
- Drinking straws
- Tape
- Construction paper (optional)

Directions

1. Choose a Ride template and color the pieces. Then cut them out and glue them to the side of your box. (Don't worry; you can always download and print more from my website for your next project.)

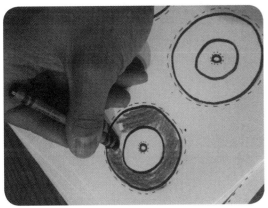

2. For wheels for the train, color and cut out the wheels and the wheel tabs.

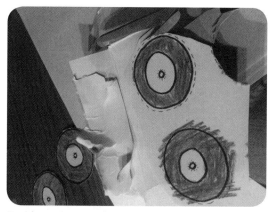

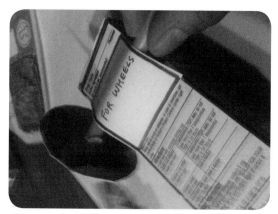

3. Glue the wheels (*not* the tabs) to the cardboard and cut them out. Poke the hole for the straws.

4. Tape the tabs to the bottom of the box. Stick the straws through the wheels.

Now you're ready to hit the road!

You Can Also Do This

Take the box and place it on a piece of copy paper or construction paper, and tape one end of it to the box. Then fold the paper around the box, as if you were gift-wrapping it. Cut off the excess and tape it down. Now glue the template pieces and draw more details.

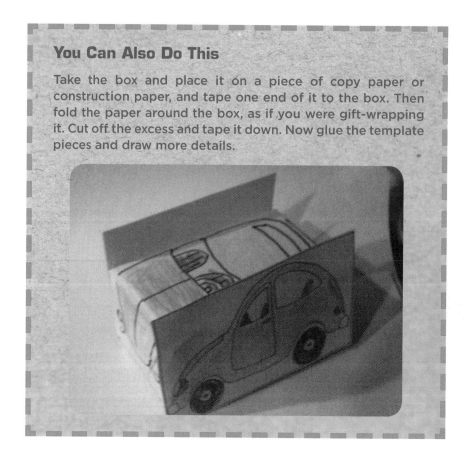

Your Neighborhood

One of my favorite childhood memories is watching *Mister Rogers' Neighborhood.* Not only did I love it when he set up the Neighborhood of Make-Believe, but also *his* neighborhood was a series of model houses the camera would pan around.

Start collecting boxes to build *your* own neighborhood. You can have a steady flow of traffic using the vehicles from Planes, Trains, and Automobiles (see Ride templates, pages 147–50). You can also make new neighbors with the Little People templates (pages 143–45).

Materials

- Neighborhood templates (pages 151–54)
- Crayons/markers
- Scissors
- Various empty cartons, boxes, and containers
- Glue
- Construction paper (optional)

Directions

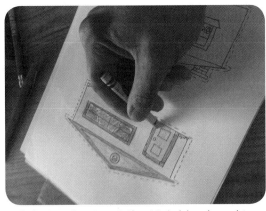

1. Color and cut out the Neighborhood templates.

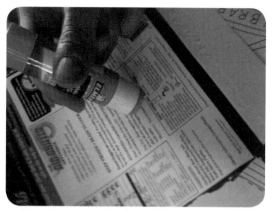

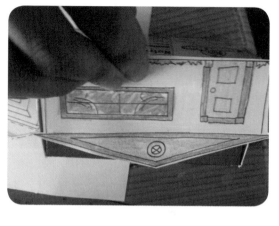

2. Glue them to the boxes.

3. Set them up and take a walk around the block.

You Can Also Do This

You can always go to my website and download more of the Neighborhood templates, but go ahead and try creating some yourself, freehand. Wrap construction paper around the boxes (trimming off any excess), and add doors, windows, and other features. *Everyone* is an artist, and some of the most imaginative ones are architects.

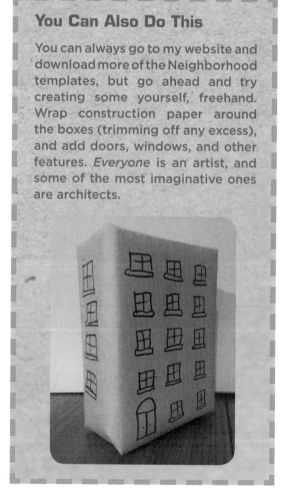

Drum

How could you *not* turn any round container into a drum? It's the perfect shape, and all you need to do is keep the beat!

Materials

- Empty round container with lid (for example, oatmeal or ice cream container)
- Construction paper
- Tape
- Scissors
- Crayons/markers
- Chopsticks
- Buttons, ribbon, glitter glue, string (optional)

Directions

1. Wrap a piece of construction paper around the container. Tape it down and trim off any excess.

2. Put the lid back on. Draw a design on the side.

3. Use the chop sticks for your drumsticks. Rat-a-tat-tat!

You Can Also Do This

Add buttons, ribbon, or glitter glue to decorate it. You can also attach a string to the drum to loop it over your shoulders. Then you can take your show on the road!

Banjo

She'll be comin' 'round the mountain to hear this tuneful instrument, and you'll be a-pickin' and a-grinnin' to a whole new beat!

Materials

- Milk carton
- Marker
- Scissors
- Rubber bands
- Duct tape
- Paper-towel tube and construction paper (optional)

Directions

1. Wash out and dry the milk container.

2. Draw a 3-by-3-inch square on one side of the carton. Cut it out.

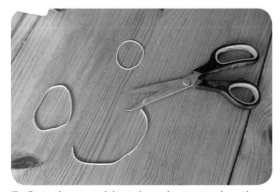

3. Cut three rubber bands to make them long in length.

4. Mark off three holes near the bottom of the cut-out area.

5. Then (the adult should) poke through them.

6. Push a rubber band through the hole and then knot the end. Repeat this for the other two holes and bands. Fold down the rubber bands on the back and tape them down.

7. Draw three lines at the top. Carefully, (the adult should) cut slits in them.

8. Feed rubber bands through the slits and knot the ends. Tape them down.

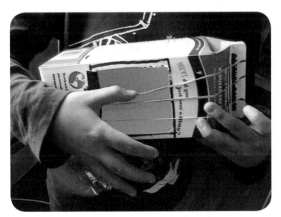

9. And a-one, and a-two, and a-three!

You Can Also Do This

Wrap construction paper around a paper-towel tube. Cut two slits at the bottom. Slip it onto the top of the milk carton and duct-tape it down to keep it in place. This becomes the "neck" of your banjo. Then, wrap construction paper around the milk carton and carefully cut out the middle (also being careful not to cut the rubber bands). Now you can decorate your banjo!

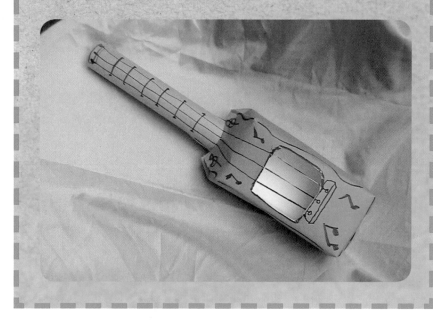

Rain Stick

It's believed that rain sticks were invented by Aztec Indians, who played them to create rain. I know yours will have the soothing sound of raindrops and will be used to make music, but you never know . . . Better keep an umbrella nearby!

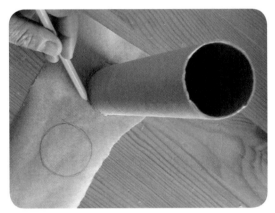

Materials

- A paper-towel or gift-wrapping tube
- Waxed paper
- Scissors
- Tape
- Dried rice
- Construction paper
- Crayons/markers

Directions

1. Trace two circles onto the waxed paper using the tube.

2. Cut out the circles, leaving about half an inch extra around the edge. Tape one circle to one end of the tube.

3. Pour half a cup of dried rice into the tube. Tape the other circle to the other end to seal in the rice.

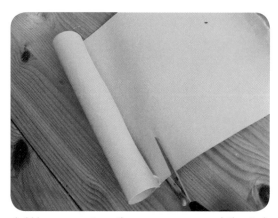

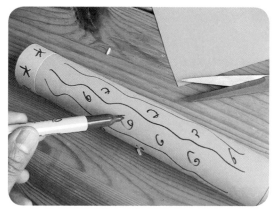

4. Wrap construction paper around the tube. Decorate it with crayons or markers.

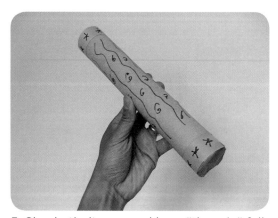

5. Slowly tip it over and hear "the rain" fall.

You Can Also Do This

Use a longer gift-wrapping paper tube for a longer-lasting "storm."

Mask #2: The Raven

This project is based on the masks created by folks from many cultures, to wear atop their heads in ceremonies and celebrations. I created a show for New York's Bronx Zoo, and one of the animal tricksters was "Raven," the star of many Pacific Northwest Native American stories. His head was made of cardboard, too (but you'd never know it).

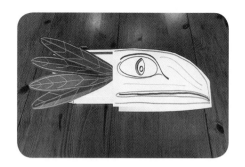

Materials

- Poster paper
- Crayons/markers
- Scissors
- Construction paper
- Stapler
- A squarish box (that can rest comfortably on one's head)
- Duct tape
- Glue (optional)

Directions

1. Fold the poster paper in half.

2. Draw a long bird's beak from one side to the folded edge. (Note: Make sure to include the folded edge.)

3. With the poster paper still folded, cut out the beak. (Note: Do *not* cut the folded edge; it keeps the beak's tip together.)

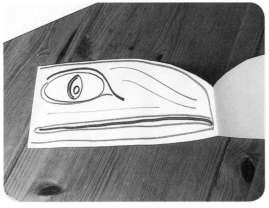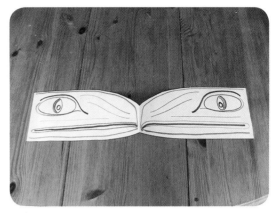

4. Draw eyes and any other features on the head.

5. Fold a piece of construction paper in half. Then fold it in half, again.

6. Draw a feather on one side. Cut it out with all the sides still folded. Now you have four feather cut-outs.

7. Draw on the rest of the feathers. Repeat the process again, to create four more.

8. Fan four of the feathers and staple them together.

9. If the box is loose on your head, fold one side of flaps down into the box.

10. Tape the four feathers to one side of the box. Flip it over and tape down the other four on the other side. You should now have feathers on either side of the box.

11. Tear off a piece of duct tape and "roll" it onto itself.

12. Place the sticky rolled piece onto the box on either side below the feathers.

13. Line up one side of the bird head and press it down onto the sticky piece. Repeat this to attach the other side.

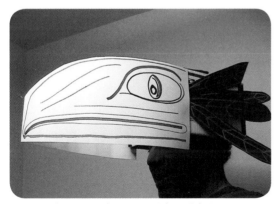

14. Put it on and crow with pride!

You Can Also Do This

My son suggested making pupils that pop. He made some out of tape and glued them onto the eyes.

You can also create other animals, such as a dinosaur and let out your best T-Rex roar!

Telescope

I spy with my little eye, something to play with made out of a paper-towel tube. This quick and easy telescope will enhance your adventures in the jungle or on the high seas.

Materials

- Construction paper
- One paper-towel tube
- Tape
- Scissors
- Crayons/markers, glitter glue, stickers, etc. (optional)

Directions

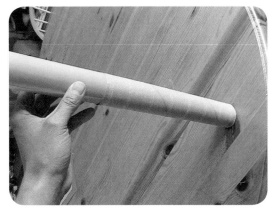

1. Roll up a piece of construction paper and then feed it into the end of the tube, so that it fits snugly.

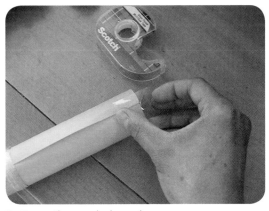

2. Tape the end closed.

3. Roll another piece of construction paper around the paper-towel tube.

 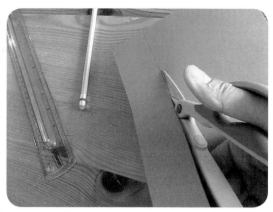

4. Cut two strips from a piece of construction paper in another color. Tape the paper strips to each end of the tube. Feed the first tube back into the second tube.

5. Now, what do *you* spy with your little eye?

You Can Also Do This

Decorate your telescope with markers, stickers, glitter glue—anything you'd like, to add that personal touch to your telescope. Or get contact paper that looks like wood and wrap it around the tubes to give it a nautical look.

» CHAPTER TWO «

Medium-Size Boxes

To me, medium-size boxes are typically larger than a cereal box but smaller than a box that would hold an oven or another large appliance. They are the boxes we receive in the mail when we order items online: shipped toys, books, electronics, and even clothes, to name a few.

These boxes are usually made of stiffer cardboard, so you may need to use a box cutter for some of them. (Note: An adult should always be in charge of the box cutter.) And remember: Keep the leftover cardboard; it's great to have on hand whenever you need "scrap cardboard" for other projects.

So let's get started!

Magic Box

I remember reading a book about magic tricks as a kid and thinking, "Maybe I could make that." And I did! I even used it as inspiration for a script I wrote for the Nick Jr. show, *Gullah Gullah Island.* Now you, too, can be a master of prestidigitation! (That means, get ready to work your magic.)

Materials

- A medium-size box
- Construction paper
- Glue
- Scissors
- Wrapping paper or gift bag
- Crayons/markers

Directions

1. Flatten the box.

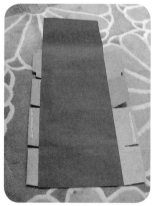

2. Glue down a long piece (or line up several separate pieces) of construction paper.

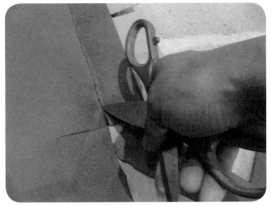 

3. Using the blade tip of the scissors, gently cut off any excess paper on the flaps.

4. Take another piece of construction paper of the same color, and the same width and length of one of the box's sides, and fold up each side (about ½ inch).

5. Add glue to the turned-up sides.

6. Glue it, folded side down, to the inside of the box to make a "secret pocket."

7. Refold and glue the box back together with construction-paper side facing in. (Adjust and re-glue the paper near the end if you have to.) Glue the end closed.

8. Use wrapping paper or a gift bag and cut out stars and moons.

9. Glue them onto the box.

10. Take a small piece of construction paper and fold it in half.

11. Draw a rabbit on one side. Cut it out with the paper still folded so you end up with two rabbit shapes.

12. Draw the exact same features on both so you have twin rabbits.

Now you're ready to do the magic trick below!

You Can Also Do This

The Magic Trick

1. Before you begin, put both rabbits in your pocket.

2. Open the box and tilt it so that the audience can see it's empty (making sure the flap is low enough to cover the secret pocket).

3. Put the box down (with the secret pocket toward you). Pick up the (one) rabbit and tell your audience how this bunny can never stay in one place for long—it's always disappearing!

4. Put the rabbit into the box (but you are really putting it in the secret pocket).

5. Close it. Then jerk it around as if the rabbit were hopping inside. Say that it's trying to get out.

6. Then suddenly stop the movement. Open the box and look in, saying, "Oh no—not again!"

7. Tilt the box the same way you did before to show that the rabbit is gone (but with the flap slightly folded, so it still hides the secret pocket and keeps the first bunny from falling out).

8. Then start squirming. Say that it feels like something is in your pocket. Then . . .

9. Reach in and pull out the "other" rabbit, saying, "He just won't stay in his box!"

Balloon Tennis

This is always a stormy-day favorite at our house. Once you push back the furniture, make sure to keep the balloon from touching the floor. The best part? When you play tennis with paddles made from boxes and a balloon for a ball, you don't have to worry about damaging anything.

Materials

- Plate (dinner-size) or large lid from a pot
- Stiff scrap cardboard or medium-size box
- Scissors
- Crayons/markers
- Ruler
- Two paper-towel tubes
- Duct tape
- One balloon
- Masking or painter's tape (optional)

Directions

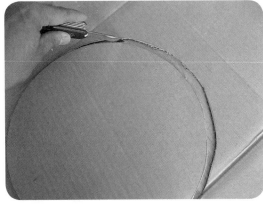

1. Take the plate or lid and trace two circles onto the box or scrap cardboard. Cut them out.

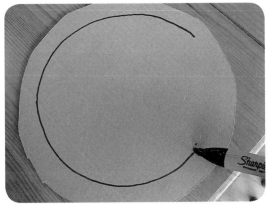

2. Draw a circle inside each and some "netting" (lines crisscrossing each other) for your paddle.

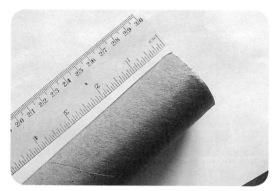

3. Measure off 2 inches from one end of a paper-towel tube, on each side. Snip them. Repeat with the other tube. Hold onto the larger pieces; they will be the handles for your paddle.

4. Line up the tube end to the bottom of a circle. Draw two lines on the paper-towel tube to indicate each side. Cut the lines.

5. Slip a circle onto the slits of a tube and tape it onto the circle. Repeat with the other circle.

6. Blow up the balloon and serve!

You Can Also Do This

Make another pair of paddles for a game of doubles. Mark off where the net and boundaries would be with masking (or blue painter's) tape, or two chairs.

Note: Duct tape now comes in many colors so you can use it to decorate and not just attach.

Building Blocks

You *could* buy cardboard building blocks—but why not save money and recycle what you already have to make your own? This project is so easy: Just collect various boxes to make blocks for stacking, building, and, of course, knocking over!

Materials

- Boxes of various sizes
- Packing tape
- Box cutter
- Crayons/markers (optional)

Directions

1. Seal up the ends of the boxes with packing tape. Then . . .

2. Cut the boxes into two triangles: Draw a diagonal line across the sides of a box (both lines going in the same direction, of course).

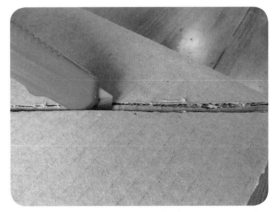

3. Cut and separate the halves. (Note: An adult should be in charge of the box cutter.)

4. Use scrap cardboard to complete the sides.

5. Now, start building.

6. And then, knock 'em down!

You Can Also Do This

You can use crayons or markers to draw letters, numbers, even bricks, on the sides of the boxes.

Hit-or-Miss

This is a classic shooting game that you'd find at a carnival. If you'd like to set up your own midway of games, definitely have your customers try their luck with this one. You may even want to practice to improve your own chances of getting the paper ball through the holes. (Plus, it's a great way to boost your child's hand-eye coordination and motor skills.)

Materials

- Bathroom-tissue tube
- Ruler
- Scissors
- Scrap cardboard
- Rubber band (small)
- A medium-size cardboard box (or large cereal box)
- A cup
- Crayons/markers
- Scrap paper
- Construction paper, glue (optional)

Directions

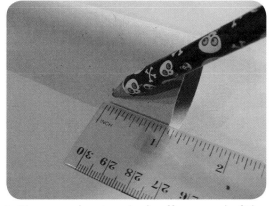

1. Measure about an inch off one end of the bathroom-tissue tube and mark a dot on each side.

2. Poke a hole through each dot.

 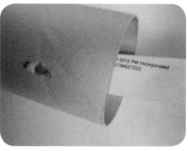 

3. Cut out a small rectangle from the scrap cardboard. (Note: It should be able to slide in and out of the tube with ease.) Dot it and poke a hole through it.

 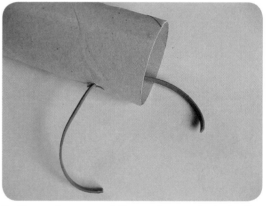

4. Cut the rubber band in half.

5. Thread one end through one hole in the tube, through the hole in the rectangle, and then through the other hole in the tube.

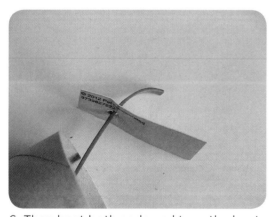 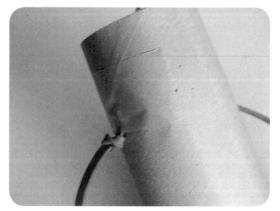

6. Then knot both ends and tape the knots down. Your "cannon" is ready.

7. Using the cup, draw four circles on the box.

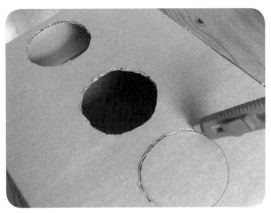

8. Cut them out. Open the bottom of the box (to allow the paper ball to roll out).

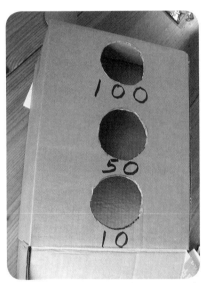

9. Assign a point value to each hole. Stand the box up.

10. Crumple up a small piece of scrap paper that can fit in the bathroom-tissue tube. (Note: Not too small that it falls out, or too big that it gets stuck.)

11. Tilt the tube up, drop in the paper ball, pull back the tab, and release it to shoot!

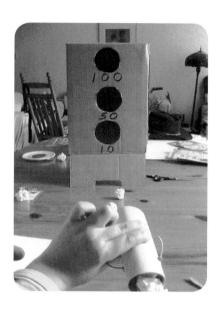

You Can Also Do This

You can decorate your Hit-or-Miss game with a volcano, ship, castle, or any target you like. Draw your creation on construction paper and then glue it to the box. Then cut out the holes and mark the value of each key spot of attack.

Mystery Box

This is a game for all ages: Just put anything in the box and have others reach in and try to guess what it is! This is especially fun when you have a group of kids over; they will be equally entertained whether they're figuring out what to put in the box or guessing what's inside.

Materials

- A box
- Crayons/markers
- Box cutter
- A cloth napkin or paper towel
- Duct tape
- Paint (optional)

Directions

1. Draw a circle on the side of the box, just large enough for a hand to slip in and out. Then . . .

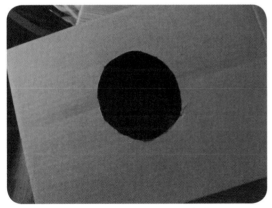

2. Use the box cutter to carefully cut out the circle.

3. Open the top and slip the napkin or paper towel in. Tape it to the top of the inside of the box so it covers the hole from the inside.

4. Place an item inside and close the top.

5. Now, take a guess!

You Can Also Do This

To add to the mystery, you can paint the box with stars, moons, and swirls. Or for a version that's ready for Halloween night, paint it all black (but I'm "guessing" you already knew that).

Dollhouse

I love this one; it's so quick and easy, and you can just keep adding to it—just like you do with a real home!

Materials

- One medium-size (or slightly larger) box
- Scissors
- Duct tape
- Dollhouse templates (pages 155–59)
- Crayons/markers
- Tape
- Glue
- Little People templates (pages 143-45)
- Paint, chalk (optional)

Directions

1. Un-tape the box. Let the flaps fall open.

2. Cut off the long flaps of the box's open end.

3. Flip up the top-side flaps of the top and connect them with duct tape to make a "roof." Let the bottom ones fall flat.

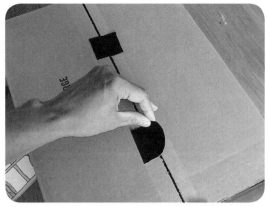

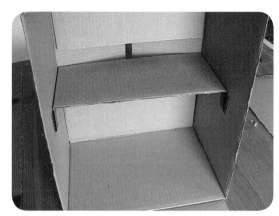

4. Duct-tape one end of the box closed. This will be the front of your house.

5. Take one of the long flaps that you've cut off the box and line it up across the inside, to make a second floor; if needed, fold the sides to fit it in and duct-tape it in place.

6. Color and cut out the windows, doors, and furniture templates.

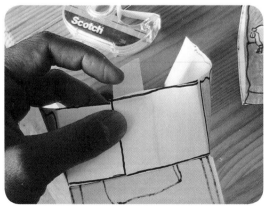

7. Tape the furniture together and glue the doors and windows.

8. Line up and cover the duct tape on the front of the house with the outside door and windows.

9. Glue all of the inside pieces to the inside of the house.

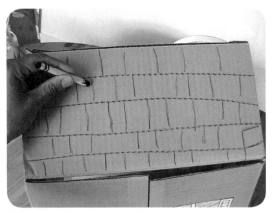

10. Draw lines across the roof to make "shingles." Then draw a rectangle in front of the door (on the bottom flap) for a "welcome mat."

11. Now, make some "new friends" with the Little People templates or use any small toys around and make yourself at home!

You Can Also Do This

For a more eerie abode, especially around Halloween, paint the house black and color in the house templates with gray markers. Then use chalk to draw the shingles and any other details for a frightful makeover. Boo!

Sword and Shield

What would a knight be without a sword and shield to defend the realm and slay vicious monsters? A walking, talking tin can! ("Joust" kidding.) This sword isn't found in a stone, but the shield *can* come with pepperoni.

Materials

- The top of a large pizza box (not the greasy bottom)
- Crayons/markers
- Box cutter (if needed; for adult use only)
- Scissors
- Glue
- Aluminum foil
- Cardboard
- Duct tape
- Shield Symbol template (pages 160–61)
- Medium-size box
- Ruler
- Crayons/markers
- Velcro, baseball cap, feather (optional)

Directions

1. Using the lid from a big pot, trace a large circle on the top of a large pizza box. Cut it out.

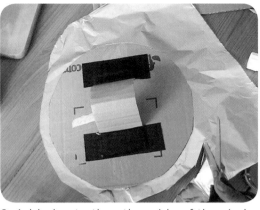 

2. Add glue to the other side of the circle and lay it onto aluminum foil. Cut around the foil leaving about an inch. Add glue to the edges and press the foil down onto it. Cut out a rectangular piece of cardboard for an arm and tape the sides down.

3. Color and cut out the Shield Symbol template and glue it to the front.

4. Measure off two lines, each 12 inches in length and 3 inches apart. Mark 3 inches across the line. Draw a "curve" connecting the lines at the top. At the other end, mark across 6 inches. Draw the handle (aka, the "cross guard," the "grip," and the "pommel").

 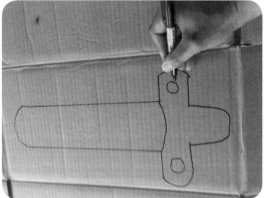

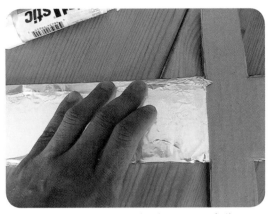

5. Cut the sword out and then trace it onto another piece of cardboard and cut that one out, too. Glue them together.

6. Cover the blade with aluminum foil.

7. Now, have at thee!

You Can Also Do This

Make a helmet. Draw a long rectangle with triangled curved ends onto a piece of cardboard and cut it out. Cut out the slats and cover it all in tin foil. Add Velcro to each side and attach it to the back of a baseball hat. Then, cover the cap in foil and add a construction paper feather.

Toy Theater

Toy theaters have been around since the early 1800s. They were made out of paper, sold as kits, taken home, put together, and used for performances. They are still around today. Create this one, and then, "The play's the thing!"

Materials

- A long, flat box (free at your local US post office)
- Ruler
- Box cutter
- Construction paper
- Crayons/markers
- Drinking straws (the kind with the bendy end)
- Tape
- Waxed paper and flashlight (optional)

Directions

1. Measure off 1 inch from each side of the front (or back) of the box, and then two inches from the top. Cut this out. (Note: You may want to slip a small cutting board underneath to prevent cutting through the other side of the box.)

2. Measure off ¼ inch from the top edge. Then measure ¼ inch from this line. This will be the curtain slot. Use the box cutter to cut out this long, thin rectangle.

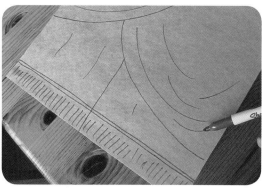

3. Slip a piece of construction paper down into the slot to make sure it fits. Then remove it.

4. Draw a "curtain" on the paper (lines and "fringe" on the bottom).

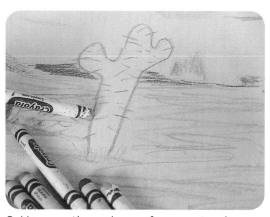

5. Decorate your theater any way you'd like.

6. Use another piece of paper to draw a "backdrop" (the background for your play).

7. Slip the backdrop into the box.

8. Snip a straw into two pieces. Tape a piece to the top of the curtain, on either side. Slip the curtain back down into the slot. Now you can raise the curtain and let it hang off the back.

9. Draw, color, and cut out any characters you want. If the paper is thin, glue the character to lightweight scrap cardboard and cut it out.

10. Tape the bendy end of a drinking straw to a character. This way you can turn it left or right for your character to enter from either side.

11. Curtain up! It's show time!

You Can Also Do This

Use the piece you cut out of the front to do the same to the back. Tape a piece of waxed paper to the inside of the box. Shine a flashlight behind it, and now you have a shadow theater!

Treasure Chest

I made this for my son's birthday, which featured a pirate theme and a treasure hunt. Now we use it to store all his schoolwork and art from kindergarten. He enjoys reliving "the memories."

Materials

- One medium-size box
- Ruler
- Pencil
- Box cutter
- Crayons/markers
- Scrap cardboard
- Scissors
- Glue
- Paint (optional)

Directions

1. Measure 4 inches from the top of the box along three sides of the box. Cut along the line with a box cutter.

2. Lift and pull it back to create a hinge for the lid.

3. Draw lines to make it look like a chest.

4. Draw a "lock" on a piece of scrap cardboard and cut it out.

5. Glue the "lock" to the front of the lid.

6. Now you have a perfect place to store all of your treasures!

You Can Also Do This

You can paint the chest any color you choose. To make it look even more like a pirate's treasure chest, lift up all four top flaps and draw diagonal lines on the side flaps; cut off these triangle pieces so that the front and back flaps can rest evenly against them. Use scrap cardboard to create the top, and hot-glue all the flaps to it.

Vampire Mirror

This project is inspired by a vampire's trait (of not being able to see his own reflection), and is one of our favorite Halloween decorations. It's perfect for vampires about to step out for the evening to get a "bite."

Materials

- Lightweight box (such as a large pizza box)
- Scissors
- Crayons/markers
- Glue
- Aluminum foil
- String or yarn
- Duct tape

Directions

1. Cut off the lid of a pizza box. Cut it in half and draw an oval on one side.

2. Cut it out.

3. Lay the oval on the other piece and trace around it. Then cut it out.

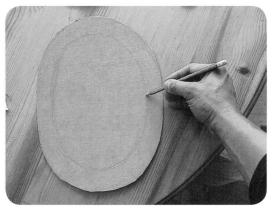 

4. Draw a smaller oval in one of the larger ones. Cut it out and add your own touches to it.

 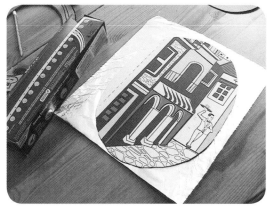

5. Apply glue to the other oval. Tear off a piece of aluminum foil and carefully lay the oval, glue-side down, onto it.

6. Flip it over and fold back the foil.

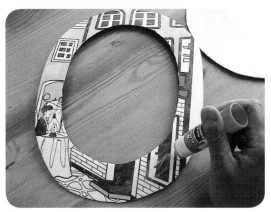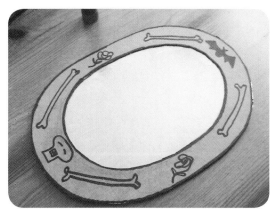

7. Apply glue around the edge of the oval frame. Lay it down onto the foiled oval.

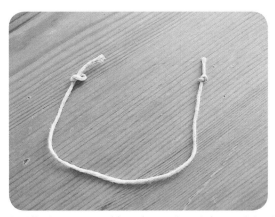

8. Flip it over and lay the string (about 6 inches in length) on the back, near the top. Knot both ends and duct-tape it down.

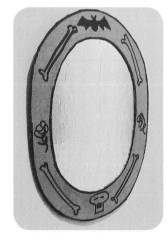

9. Now, hang it up and get a good look at yourself . . . so to speak.

You Can Also Do This

You can make a smaller one as a hand mirror to take with you.

Mini Golf

I love mini golf. (There; I said it.) It's fun and easy to play mini golf (or "putt-putt," as it's sometimes called) at home or in the yard. Just line up the shot, address the ball ("Hello, ball"), and . . . FORE!

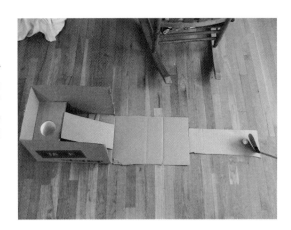

Materials

- One medium-size box
- Box cutter
- Cup
- Hot glue gun
- Pencil
- Duct tape
- Scrap cardboard
- Scissors
- Wooden dowel or a straight wooden stick (24 to 36 inches in length)
- Aluminum foil

Directions

1. Open up the top of the box. Cut the front end and let the side and its flap fall open.

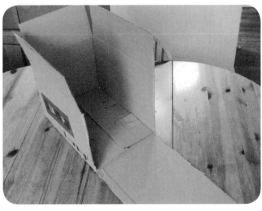

2. Cut off the four flaps from one side of the box. Flip the box over.

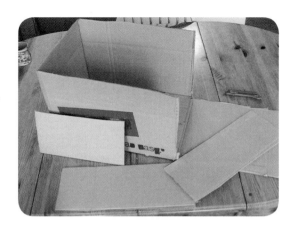

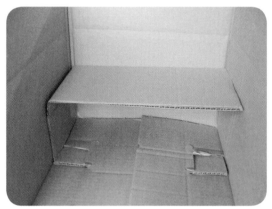

3. Use one of the long flaps for the shelf inside. Bend it and slip it in to make sure it's a snug fit.

4. Use the cup to trace a circle at the top of the shelf and cut it out.

5. Tape the cup to the hole. Flip it over and slide it into the box. Hot glue it down.

6. Tape one of the shorter flaps down and then lift it up toward the cup. This is the ramp.

7. Tape down the other short flap to the front in order to extend the length of your "fairway."

 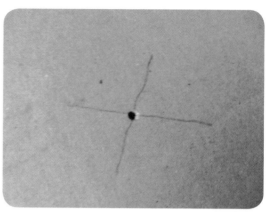

8. Mark an "X" at the end and then poke the center with a pencil. This will be your "tee," to keep the ball from rolling.

9. Line up the stick with the scrap card-board and draw the end of a "golf club" (think egg-shape/oval).

10. Cut it out and duct-tape it to the wooden dowel (or stick).

11. Ball up a wad of aluminum foil to make a golf ball.

12. Now, go for that hole in one!

You Can Also Do This

You can streamline your mini golf "course" and make it even longer, and you can also add a "ball return." Connect cardboard to the bottom of the cup (or bowl, to give the ball more of a spin) and out to the side of the box, at an angle; then the ball will roll back to you.

Marble Madness

Yes, this is a basic lesson in gravity, but it's also just downright fun to see those marbles roll!

Materials

- Medium-size box
- Scissors
- Two paper-towel tubes
- Pencil
- Duct tape
- Marbles

Directions

1. Cut off three flaps of the box.

2. Cut the paper-towel tubes in half to get four "slides" for the marbles to roll through.

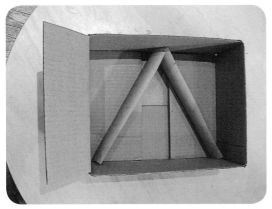

3. Start to fit them in the box to see how long and short they need to be in order for the marble to roll from one to another. If you need to shorten a slide, do so.

4. Draw a circle near a top corner of the box. Cut it out.

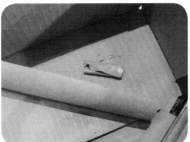

5. Roll duct tape. Lift a paper-towel tube and stick the rolled tape to the back of the box. Press the tube down on it. Repeat for the other tubes.

6. Use one tube for the "exit ramp." Put tape on one end and stick it to the back of the box, near the bottom. Make sure its edge is against the side (to keep the marble from missing it and falling). Let the other end drop.

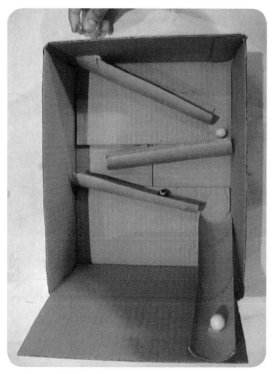

You Can Also Do This

You can keep adding more tubes and boxes to create a marvelous marbling roller coaster.

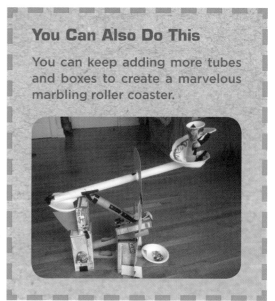

7. Now, drop a marble and watch it roll!

Horse

Saddle up, cowpoke, and giddy up toward fun adventures out west (or in your living room).

Materials

- Medium-size box (that a child can comfortably take on and off)
- Box cutter (and cutting board)
- Pencil
- Ruler
- Crayons/markers
- Duct tape
- Measuring tape (or string)
- Construction paper
- Paint (optional)

Directions

1. Cut off all four bottom flaps and the top flaps.

2. Take one of the short flaps and measure off about 3 to 4 inches from the top. Do the same to one of the long flaps, measuring 3 to 4 inches from the side.

 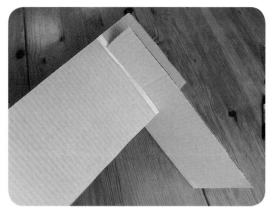

3. Cut into the lines. These are now "slots" to fit the horse's head together. Slip them together.

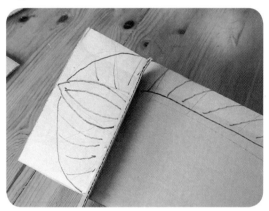 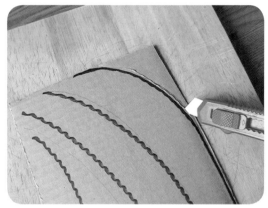

4. With the pieces in place, draw an ear and "mane" on the top and side of the long flap.

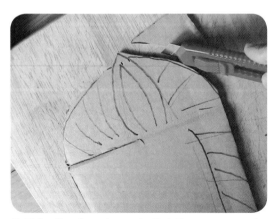 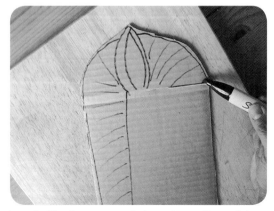

5. Take the head apart. Cut the mane and neck out, flip it over, and draw the other side.

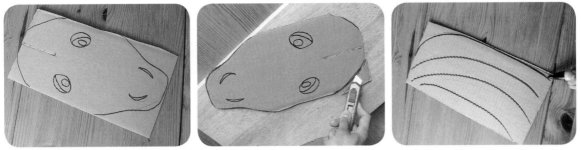

6. Draw the front of a horse's head on the short flap and a horse's tail on the other short flap. Cut them out.

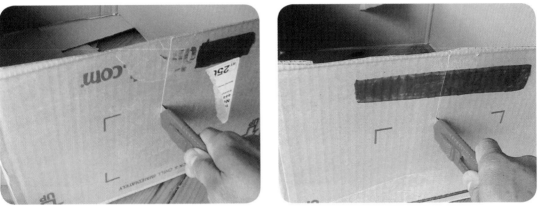

7. Cut a 3- to 4-inch slot in the front of the box. Cut a 2-inch slot at the back of the box.

8. Measure and cut a 3- to 4-inch slot near the bottom of the horse's neck. Slide it into the front slot.

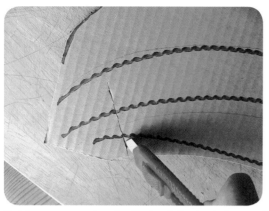 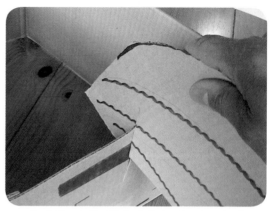

9. Measure and cut a 3- to 4-inch slot near the end of the tail. Slide it into the back slot.

 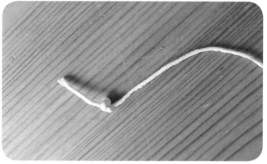

10. Cut a piece of string long enough to hang comfortably over your child's shoulders. Knot the ends. Cut the same length again, and knot it.

 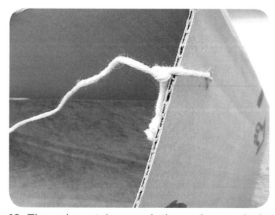

11. Carefully poke four holes: two in front on either side, and two in back, on either side.

12. Thread a string end through one hole and tie it off. Then feed it through the hole in front of it (at the other end of the box) and tie it off. These are the "shoulder straps."

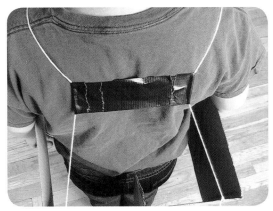

13. Pull off a long piece of duct tape. Attach it to one string, then the other. Tear off another piece to put over it.

14. Cut a long piece of string off and tie the ends together.

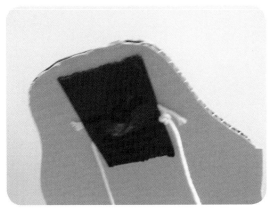

15. Tape the string to the horse, under its "chin." Slip the head back onto the head piece.

16. Hi-ho, Boxy! Away!

You Can Also Do This

Paint the horse and add detail to the head and tail with construction paper. You can even add a saddle.

» CHAPTER THREE «

Those Really BIG Boxes

So now we have come to the "classic" part of the book, meaning those really BIG boxes that furniture and appliances often arrive in, suitable for making any type of fort or castle. I remember having my castle as a kid, and years later, creating an entire empire for my son.

Because they are big, you can use these boxes in so many ways, even in their natural form. One day it's a fire truck, and then, just by opening up each end . . . Voilà! It's a tunnel leading into a cave. These big boxes provide the prime opportunity for "instant play." Just get in and start playing, over and over again.

If you want to create something specific, here are a few suggestions of what you can do. Of course, it depends on the size and shape box you have; that's a given. Just think of these examples as a jumping-off point for your imagination.

Blast Off!

Get a large-enough box, and you can imagine solo voyages into space. If you're lucky, you may even have enough room for a crewman to join you on your journey, to a realm where no box has gone before.

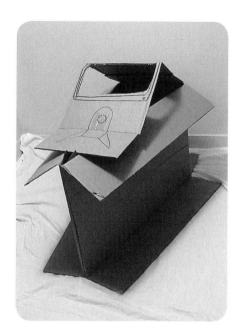

Materials

- One large box
- Box cutter
- Hot glue gun and glue sticks
- Crayons/markers
- Paper-towel tubes (optional)

Directions

1. Find the connecting side of the box (that flap of cardboard attached to one side) and pull it apart.

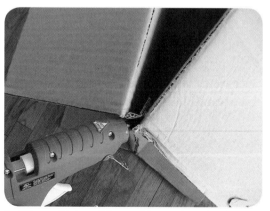

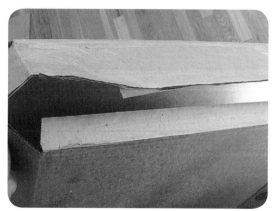

2. Slice off the side and hot-glue the box back together to form a triangle.

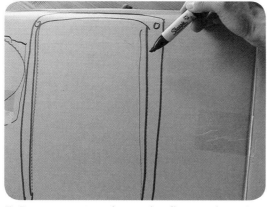

3. Draw a rectangle on the flap and cut it out.

4. Take the side and hot-glue it to the back. This is now the lid to your rocket ship. Lift it up and climb in. All systems go?

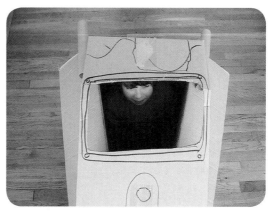

5. BLAST OFF!

You Can Also Do This

Add any details you like, including these "thrusters" (also known as paper-towel tubes) to the sides.

Castle

I love this one. It was created one day when a neighbor's child had all these boxes, and she and my son dragged them down to our apartment to see what we could create with them. And lo, the castle stronghold arose!

Materials

- One large box
- Crayons/markers

Directions

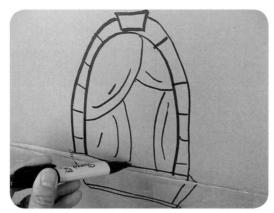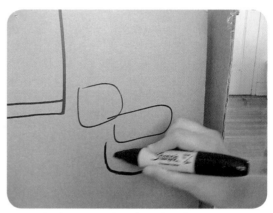

1. Open up the ends, stand it up, and draw stones, windows, and a drawbridge.

Now, you're ready to rule your kingdom!

You Can Also Do This

Get smaller boxes, open the ends, cut out windows, and just slip them onto the side of the castle to create towers.

Draw a drawbridge, cut it out, and let the flap fall onto the floor. Poke holes on either side of the opening. Thread a piece of string through one hole, knot it, and thread it through the hole near the opening. Then, thread the end through the other hole and down to the last hole. Knot it.

Now you can enter and close up your castle at will.

Desk

This is a project that you can do as a nice surprise for the child in your life. I made this for my son after he kept trying to sit at our desk to "do work, too, Daddy."

Materials

- Three large boxes (about 24 by 14 by 18 inches)
- Pencil
- Scissors or box cutter
- Ruler
- Velcro
- Duct tape
- Contact paper (optional)

Directions

1. Flatten one of the boxes and set it aside. The other two will be the sides of the desk.

2. Fold down all the flaps of each of the other two boxes, except for one on each box.

3. Fold that flap back and draw a line across the closed flaps where it lays.

4. Now lift it up and measure about an inch down from the line you drew (toward the flap end). Then cut along the *new, second* line, removing the excess.

5. Attach Velcro above the opening on each side. Peel back the sticky end and press the flap onto it. Now this "secret drawer" can open and close!

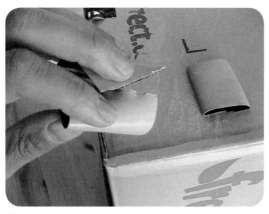

6. Arrange each side box so that they are on their sides with the flap facing out and one side facing up. Tear off a strip of duct tape and roll it into itself. Attach it to the top of a side box. Repeat three more times; now each side box has two rolled up duct tape pieces on either end.

7. Now, lay the flattened box onto the two side boxes.

8. Time to get down to business!

You Can Also Do This

Cover the desk with self-adhesive shelf paper that resembles wood. Now you have a mini mahogany workplace!

Puppet Stage

I'm a puppeteer. My love for this art form started when I was a kid. I made my own puppets and would perform shows for family and friends, eventually performing at birthday parties. So how could I *not* include a Puppet Stage in this book?

Materials

- A large cardboard box
- Box cutter
- Crayons/markers
- Bedsheet
- Two binder clips

Directions

1. You can use the entire box if you'd like, but if you want to make it easy to store when not in use, cut off one side, the top, and the bottom flaps and lay it flat.

2. Draw a large rectangle on the front side. Cut it out.

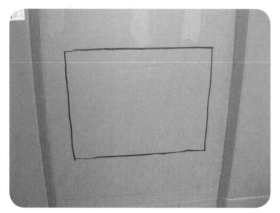

3. Let it stand and drape the sheet across the back. Use the binder clips to clip the sheet into place.

Now, on with the show!

You Can Also Do This

Decorate your Puppet Stage! This is theater, after all. Draw on it, paint on it—create whatever you want on it. Then just fold it up and store until the next performance.

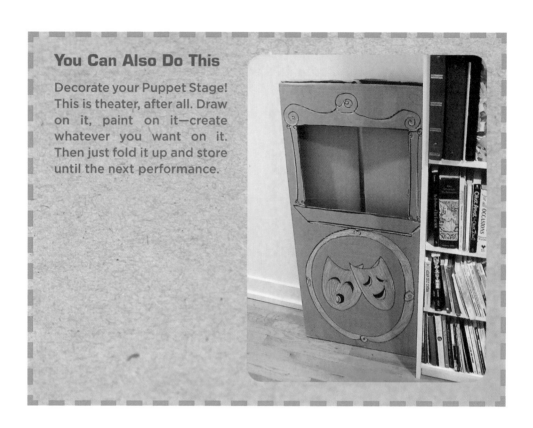

Ship Ahoy!

If you mastered building your first Pirate Ship (from page 14) and created your own Treasure Chest (from page 70), you're now ready to cast off and set sail in your very own vessel. Just open up the box and, with a few touches, you'll have this box "shipshape" in no time flat!

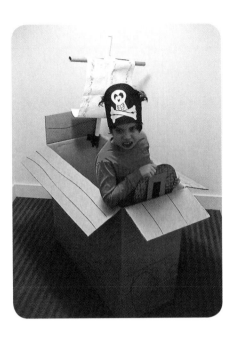

Materials

- A large box
- Gift-wrapping paper tubes
- Duct tape
- Paper towels
- Crayons/markers
- Scrap cardboard and paper fastener (optional)

Directions

1. Open the box and lay the flaps back. Make a lowercase "t" with the cardboard tubes.

2. Attach it to the back of the box by one of the flaps.

3. Tape paper towels to the "mast" to create a "sail."

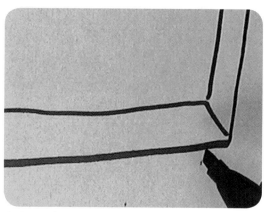

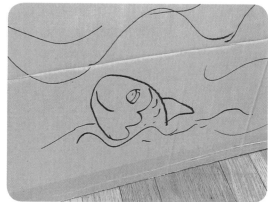

4. Draw lines on the sides (and anything else you want to add).

5. You're ready to cast off!

You Can Also Do This

You can add a wheel to steer your vessel. Take a piece of scrap cardboard and cut out a circle. Take another long rectangular piece of cardboard, place the circle on it, and punch a hole through the circle and the cardboard. Use a paper fastener (or roll up a piece of paper) and feed it through the holes in the circle and the cardboard. Flatten the fastener (or tape down one end of the rolled paper to the cardboard rectangle). Tape the cardboard to the inside front of the box. Now steer!

Remember how to make a triangle-shaped building block (see page 51)? You can adapt it to be a

proper bow for your ship. Cut the back sides open and slip it onto the front. You can even draw a mermaid masthead if you want!

Toss

Step right up! Step right up! Try your aim (with a little luck). Get a high score and win a prize (that of getting the high score).

Materials

- A large box or large flat display board (from office-supply store)
- Box cutter (if needed)
- Crayons/markers
- Small ziplock bags
- Dried rice or beans
- Tape
- Felt and gaffer tape (optional)

Directions

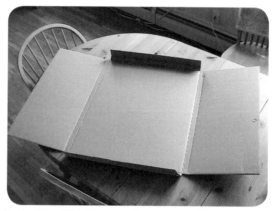

1. Flatten the box and cut out a large piece of cardboard (if you need to).

2. Draw squares on the cardboard and mark them with numbers (for point values).

3. Fill several small ziplock bags with rice and/or beans. Seal them closed with tape and decorate them.

4. Now . . . toss!

You Can Also Do This

You can cut out little pouches from felt and fill them with the rice and/or beans; then gaffer-tape the edges.

Spin the Wheel

Hurray! Hurray! Hurray! Try your luck with the wheel. Give a spin and see what happens!

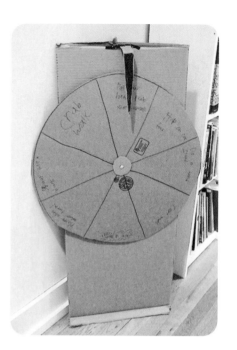

Materials

- One very large box
- Crayons/markers
- Scrap cardboard
- Box cutter
- Duct tape
- Scissors
- Paper fastener
- Dice (optional)

Directions

1. Open up the box.

 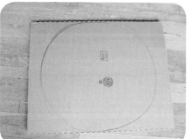 

2. On the side, draw a large circle. (If you have scrap cardboard wider than the box's side, draw the circle on it.) Cut it out.

3. Cut the box so that you have three long sides connected (as a three-fold).

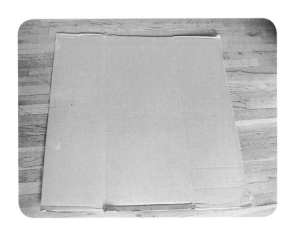

4. Fold up the sides and duct-tape them together to form a standing triangle. Stand it up.

5. To keep the triangle from tipping, cut a slight angle off at the bottom from the two back sides. Save one.

6. Cut out two small circles from scrap cardboard and punch holes through them.

7. Draw lines across the circle. Not only are these the areas for your challenges, but they also help to determine where the center point is.

8. Use the wheel to find where to poke the hole in the stand. Poke a hole at the center point.

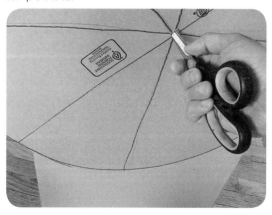

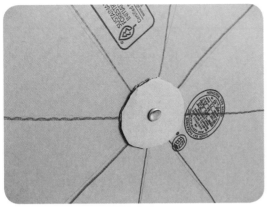

9. Thread a paper fastener through the small circle, the big wheel, and the other small circle. Push the fastener through the hole in the stand, bend the ends, and tape it down.

10. Take the one saved triangle (from the stand's bottom) and bend it. This is now the "pointer" for the wheel.

11. Add tape and attach it to the top of the stand. (Add a bit of tape to the side to keep it pointing down, if necessary.)

12. Write things to do in the wheel sections.

13. Now, spin the wheel . . . and walk like a duck!

You Can Also Do This

Spin the wheel then roll dice to see how many times you have to do a challenge. Who can hop on one foot twelve times? Can you?

Fire Truck

When my son was around four years old, he was obsessed with visiting our local firehouse. Our NYFD crew was more than patient with letting him climb inside the truck and pretend to drive. Now, your little firefighter can head off to save the day in this rig.

Materials

- A big, long box
- Crayons/markers
- Paint (optional)

Directions

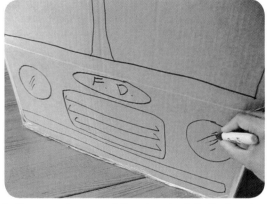

1. Draw a door and fire-truck details (such as the hoses, the wheels, dials, and so on).

2. Fold back the flap to get in and out of the truck.

3. You're ready to save the day!!!

You Can Also Do This

Of course, you can paint your truck and cut out the windows!

Playhouse

You feed them, you clothe them, you nurture them, but before you know it, your kids are moving into their own place. This playhouse depends on their (and your) imagination, so go for it!

Materials

- A really large box
- Crayons/markers
- Box cutters (optional)

Directions

1. Open up the box and see where the "doors" and "windows" can go.

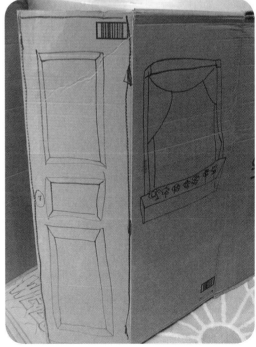

2. Now start drawing on the front and the back of the box. You can even cut out the windows.

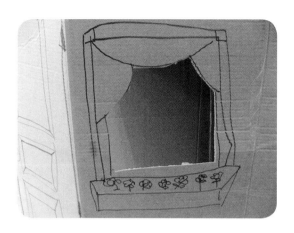

You Can Also Do This

If you have two boxes of similar size, you can fit them together for one long house. That way there's more room for parties!

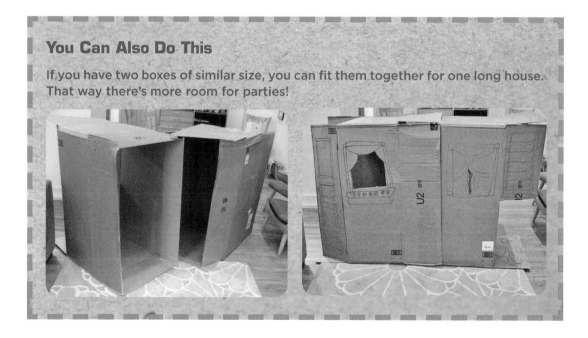

Tunnel

There's something fun, mysterious, and exciting about crawling through a box as a kid. If you don't believe me, get some that are big enough for the whole family to try.

Materials

- Several big, long boxes
- Duct tape (if needed)

Directions

1. Open up the ends of the boxes.

2. See which ones fit naturally over another; or, if they're the same size, line them up. Tape the boxes together, if necessary.

Ready . . .
set . . .
GO!

You Can Also Do This

Decorate the inside of the tunnel. You can even add the proverbial "light at the end." You can also slice into the sides of the boxes, fold them in slightly, and tape them closed. Now you have a snaky, curvy tunnel to explore.

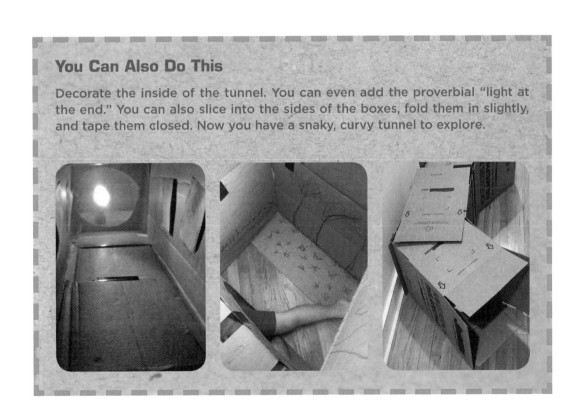

Wonderland Croquet

One of my son's favorite stories is *Alice in Wonderland.* He really wanted to play croquet, with his own hedgehog rolling through the folded cards, as if they were traditional croquet hoops You can make a date to play croquet, Wonderland style, with this set. But remember: *Always* let the Queen win.

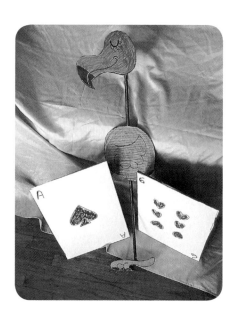

Materials

- A large box, flattened, or a large flat display board (from an office-supply store)
- Ruler
- Box cutter
- Crayons/markers
- Cardboard
- Scissors
- Duct tape
- One wooden dowel or wooden stick
- A small ball
- Construction paper (optional)

Directions

1. First, you need to make the cards. Measure off rectangles, about 12 by 16 inches in diameter. Cut them out.

2. Measure the length to find the center. Then, gently "score" (lightly cut along the line but not deep enough into it to separate the pieces) down the middle to create a fold. Bend so the "cards" stand.

3. Draw a card front, such as the three of hearts, the four of diamonds, and so on.

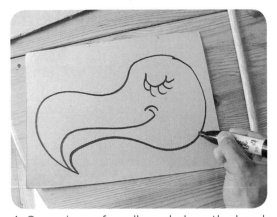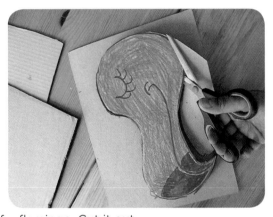

4. On a piece of cardboard, draw the head of a flamingo. Cut it out.

5. Duct-tape the head to the end of the dowel or wooden stick.

6. Draw a "body" and "feet" and cut them out. Tape them to the dowel.

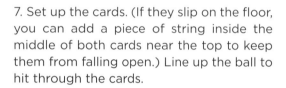

7. Set up the cards. (If they slip on the floor, you can add a piece of string inside the middle of both cards near the top to keep them from falling open.) Line up the ball to hit through the cards.

8. Let the games begin!

You Can Also Do This

You can use construction paper to add faces and feet to the cards. And if you can find one of those soft, spikey rubber balls, it makes a perfect hedgehog.

Basketball Hoop

I made this for my son when he was little, and he still plays with it today. When we can't get to the playground for a little one-on-one, he can always shoot and score from the comfort of home.

Materials

- Large cardboard box
- Box cutter
- Two wire hangers
- Pliers
- Duct tape

Directions

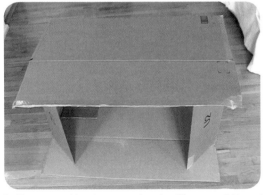

1. Open up the box and cut off one of the sides. This will be the "backboard."

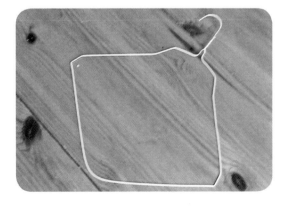

2. Take one of the wire hangers and begin to pull it open to form a circle. This will be the "hoop."

3. Cut a slit near the bottom of the card-board, but not at the edge.

4. Bend the hook of the hanger down with pliers. Feed it through the slit. Bend the hook so it is flat against cardboard.

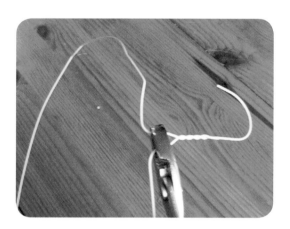

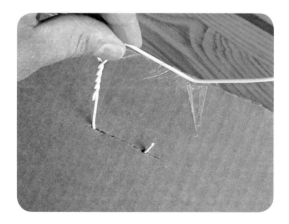

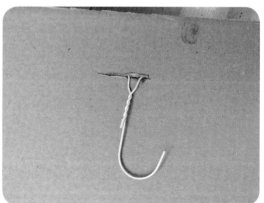

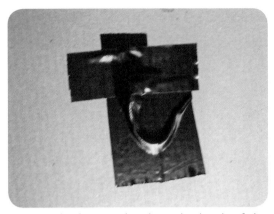

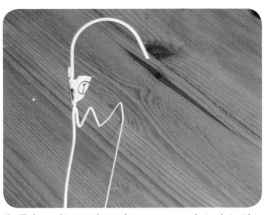

5. Tape the hanger hook to the back of the cardboard.

6. Take the other hanger and twist the hook back.

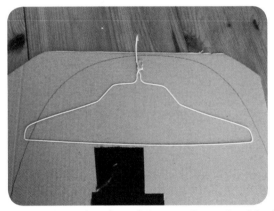

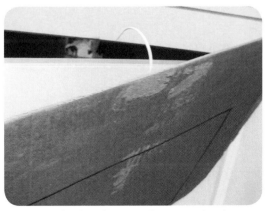

7. Tape it to the top of the cardboard, with the hook facing up.

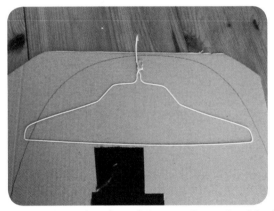

8. Cut the corners off of the cardboard, to make flat edges.

9. Place the hook onto the top of a door.

10. Now, go for the free throw!

You Can Also Do This

Create a "net" for your basketball hoop. This box happened to contain packing material that looked just like one! But you can cut strips of paper and tape them together to form a "net."

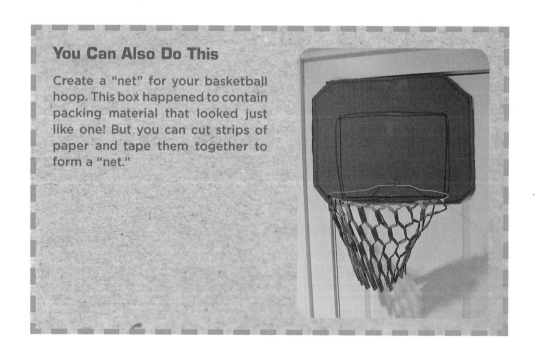

Bowling

When I was a kid, I loved watching a local bowling show on TV that had people playing for money. Yours doesn't have to be high-stakes, but you can still have fun with your own bowling set. (And you can work on your seven-ten split.)

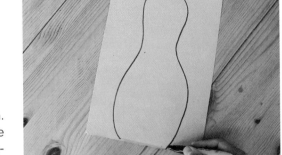

Materials

- Construction (or white copy) paper
- Crayons/markers
- Scissors
- Medium-size box
- Ruler
- Box cutter (and cutting board)
- A ball

Directions

1. On a piece of paper, draw a bowling pin. Cut it out (by folding it in half to get the sides even). This is your template for making all ten.

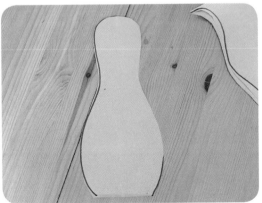

2. Flatten the box. Trace the pin on it (ten times).

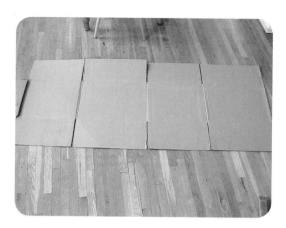

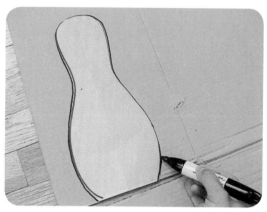

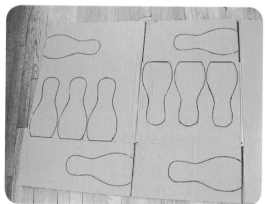

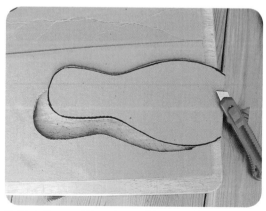

3. Put the cutting board beneath the cardboard, and cut the pins out.

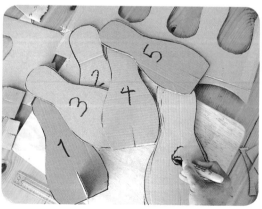

4. Write the numbers on them.

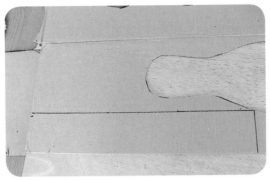
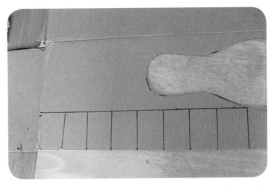

5. Draw a rectangle about 12 inches long and about 2 inches wide on a piece of cardboard. Measure off 2-inch sections along the rectangle.

6. Cut these out to be the tabs at the bottom of each pin.

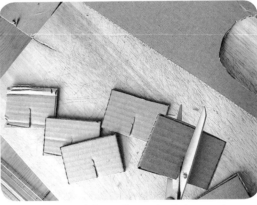

7. In the middle of each tab, make an (approximate) inch-long snip.

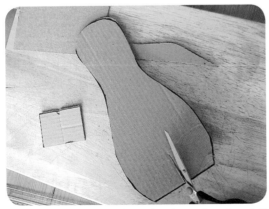

8. At the bottom of each pin, snip about 2 inches.

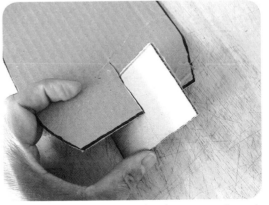

9. Slip the tabs onto the bottom of each pin to help it stand up.

10. Arrange the pins in a bowling triangle, with the number-one pin in front. Take ten steps back (or more, if you've got the room) and bowl!

You Can Also Do This

To create a theme for your bowling game, you can draw monsters, aliens, or any other creatures you can think of, with no time to "spare." (Sorry, couldn't resist.)

Kitchen

I mentioned this at the beginning of the book and it's still, fondly, one of my favorites. So make this for the aspiring chef in your family.

Materials

- Three large boxes (which can be of various sizes)
- Box cutter
- Scrap cardboard
- Crayons or markers
- Scissors
- Glue
- Velcro
- Plastic food container
- Paper fasteners
- Duct tape
- Paint (optional)

The Fridge

1. Turn the tallest box on its side and cut off one of the short flaps. Save it (for scrap cardboard).

 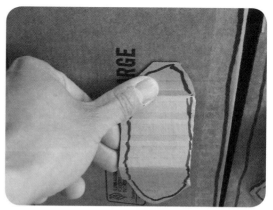

2. On scrap cardboard, draw two long ovals and cut them out. These will be the "handles" for the refrigerator. Hot glue them to each side of the box.

3. Snip of two pieces of Velcro and put one on each side of the "doors." Peel back the pieces and press them against the remaining flap, which is the "freezer."

The Sink

 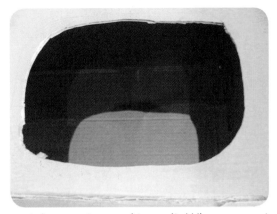

1. Flip the second box onto its side. Place the container on top and trace it. When you cut out the hole, cut *inside* the traced line. That way the container will slip into the opening but not fall through.

2. Slide the container into the hole. (You may need to trim a little of the edge to let it snuggly rest inside the opening, without falling through.)

3. From the scrap cardboard, cut out two circles. Then cut out two smaller ones. The bigger ones are the "hot" and "cold" knobs and the smaller ones are the "washers" (and you'll see why).

4. Poke two holes above the "sink" and cut a slit in between, about 2" long.

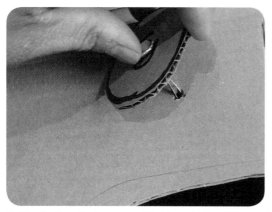

5. Push the fastener with the circles through one hole and bend back the fastener ends, from underneath.

6. On scarp cardboard, draw a "faucet" with a narrow end at the bottom. Cut it out.

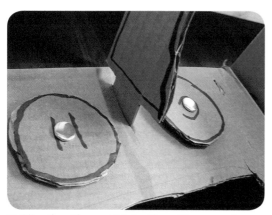
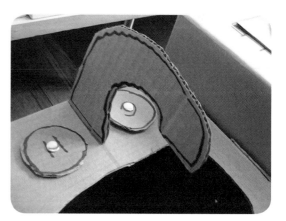

7. Slip the "faucet" into the slit you cut.

The Oven

1. Cut off the long flaps from the third box.

2. Draw a rectangle on the short flaps. Cut it out.

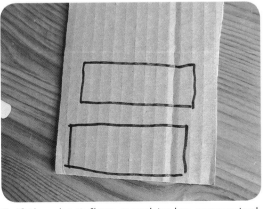 

3. If the short flaps need to be connected, draw and cut out two short rectangles. Glue them to the short flaps (to bridge the gap).

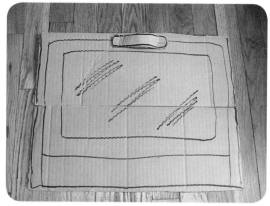

4. Tape the long flaps together. Flip it over and draw the oven "door." Cut out a long oval and glue it to the top to be the "handle."

5. Line up the "door" to the bottom of the oven and tape it.

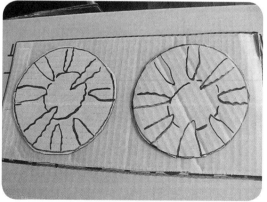

6. Glue a long cardboard to the top of the box. Trace two circles and cut them out. Glue them to the cardboard and draw the "burners" on top.

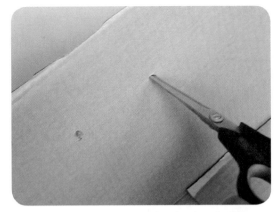

7. To connect the three boxes, line up the boxes and poke holes from the inside, from one through the other. Push paper fasteners through and bend them back. Cover with tape.

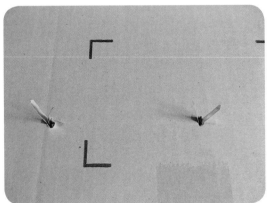

8. Now stock up with your pantry wares (from p. 10) and start cooking! (But remember to do the dishes.)

You Can Also Do This

Paint it any color you want; '70s orange or modern sleek black. You can also add shelves inside the fridge and a rack inside the oven.

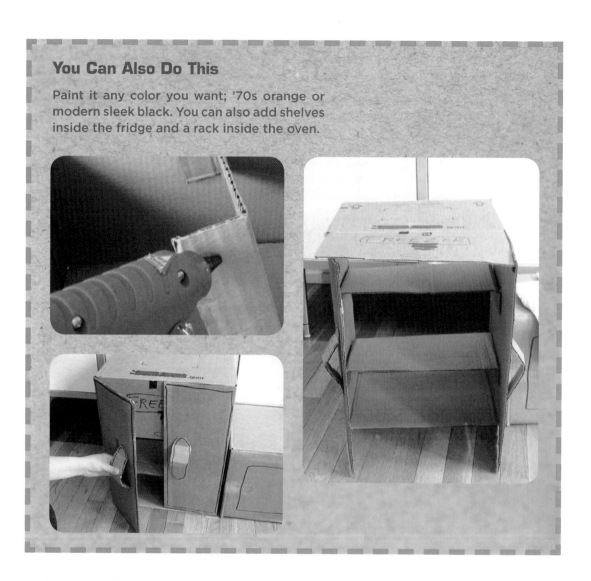

Box *Bunraku*

It's one more puppet, I know, but I couldn't help myself. I've taught so many kids, from summer camp to afterschool programs, how to make this puppet, which is based on a Japanese puppetry skill called *Bunraku.* It takes more than one person to animate this character, so gather your family members to help. (Remember: A family that plays together stays together.)

Materials

- Two boxes, one large and one slightly smaller
- Poster paper
- Crayons/markers
- Glue stick or rubber cement
- Scrap cardboard
- Scissors
- Duct tape
- Chopsticks
- Paint (optional)

Directions

1. Make sure the bottoms of both boxes are sealed; fold in the top flaps.

2. On a piece of poster paper, draw and color in a face. Glue it to the smaller box.

3. Draw a clothing design on the bigger box.

4. Cut two "handles" from scrap cardboard, about 10 inches long and 3 inches wide.

5. Take one handle and roll it around your hand to get a curve; bend the ends and hot-glue them to the inside of the smaller box.

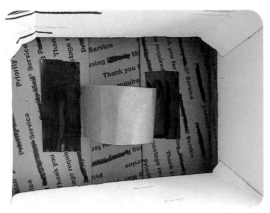

6. Then, duct-tape the handle down to make sure it stays.

7. Repeat these same steps for the bigger box.

8. Next, fold a piece of poster paper in half. Then fold it again. Cut along the creases to get four long strips.

9. Take one of the strips; fold it in half and then in half again, then again.

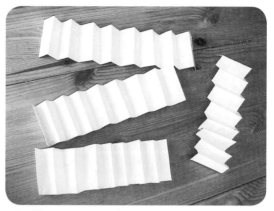

10. Then refold the strip to create an "accordion" effect. Repeat for the other three strips.

11. On scrap cardboard, draw a hand and a foot. Cut them out and then trace them. Cut the tracings out so you end up with two hands and two feet.

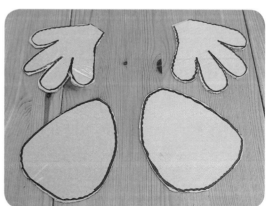

12. Tape a hand to the end of a strip. Do the same for the other hand and for each foot.

13. Lay the parts on the floor, facedown.

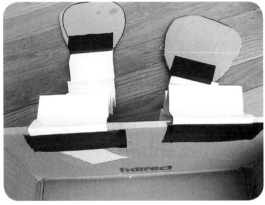

14. Duct-tape the arms to the side of the bigger box. Tape the legs to the bottom of the big box.

15. From another piece of poster paper, cut a smaller strip (half the size of the originals) and accordion it. Tape it to the bottom of the head and the top of the big box to create a "neck."

16. Tape a chopstick to the end of each hand and the bottom of each foot.

17. One person grabs the handles, another, the sticks for the hands, and one more person, the sticks for the feet.

Now, dance, puppet—DANCE!

You Can Also Do This

You can always paint your character any color(s) you want. You can also use longer wooden dowels to attach to the hands and feet.

TEMPLATES

Little People

Princess

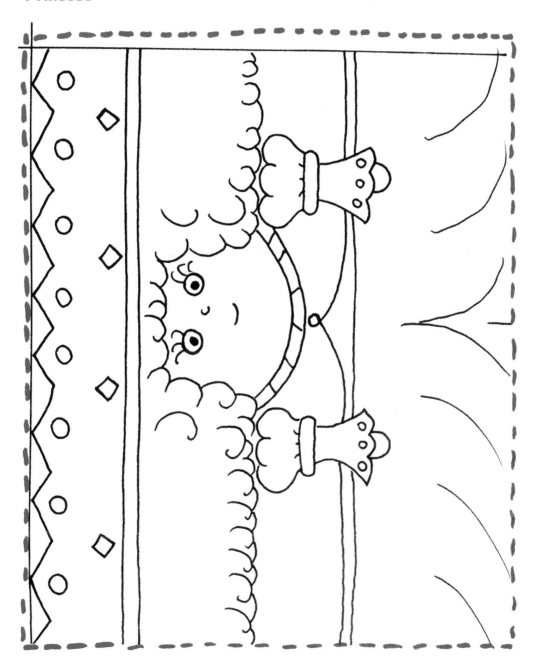

Little People

Soldier

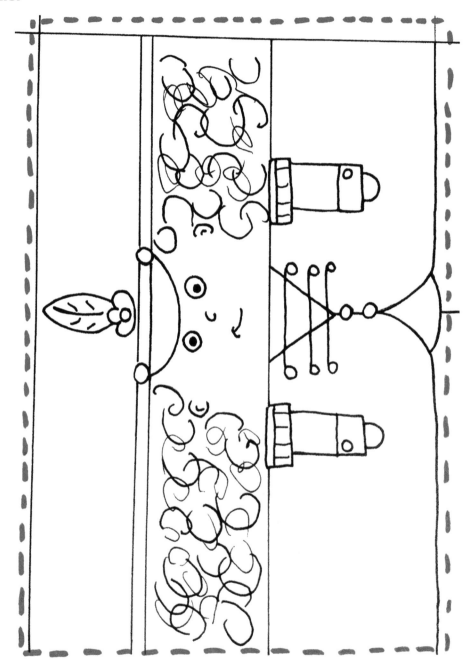

Little People

Pirate

Pirate Ship

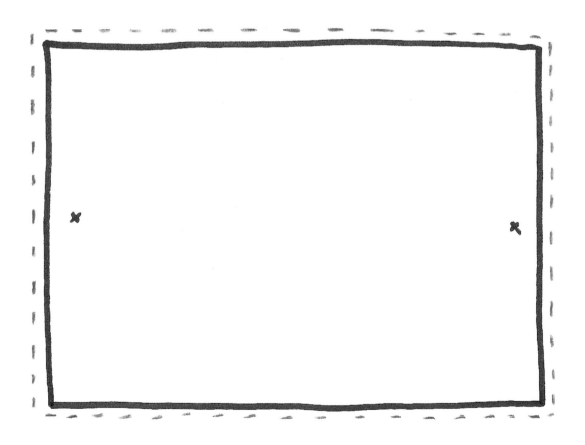

Ride

Car

Ride

Car

Ride

Train

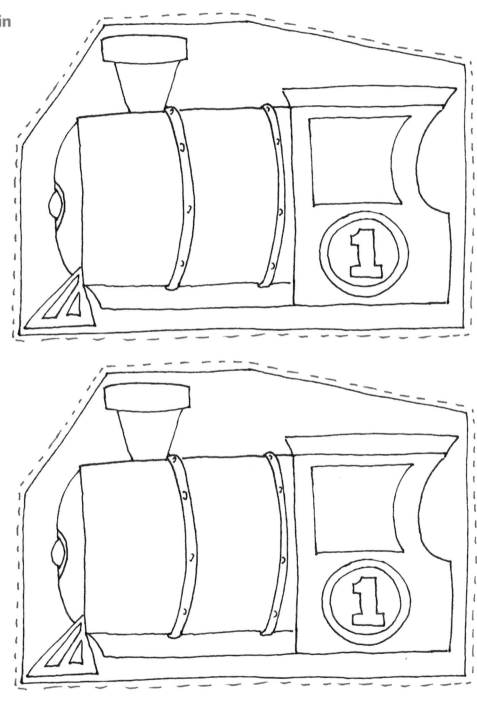

Ride

Wheels

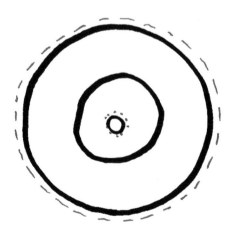

Neighborhood

Hotel

Neighborhood

Houses

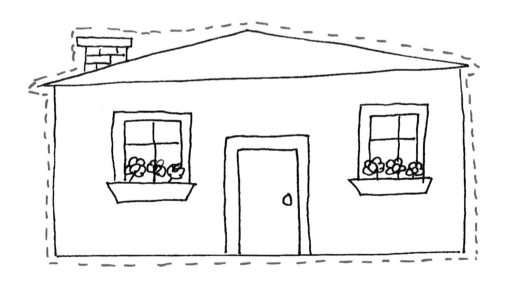

Neighborhood

Library

Neighborhood

School

Dollhouse

Bed

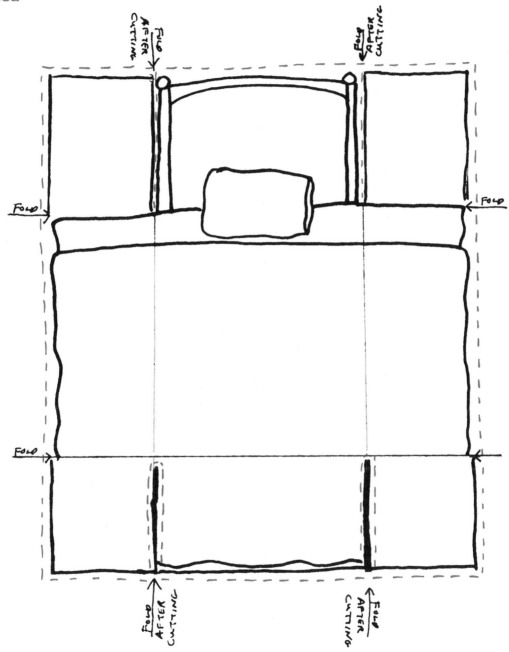

Dollhouse

Couch

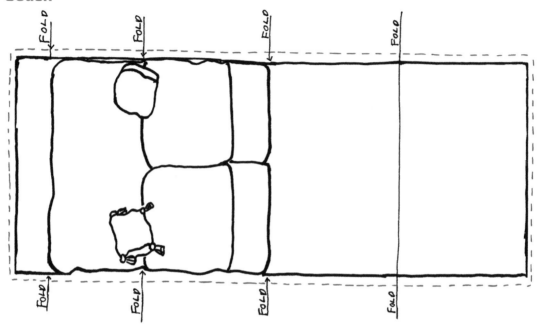

Fireplace

Dollhouse

Door 1

Door 2

Dollhouse

Dresser

Mirror

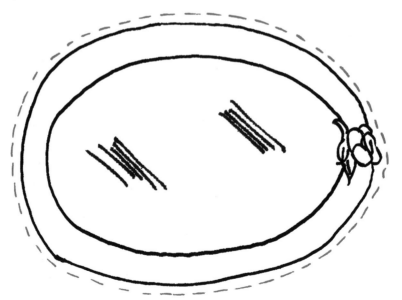

Dollhouse

Inside Window

Outside Window

Shield Symbol

Dragon

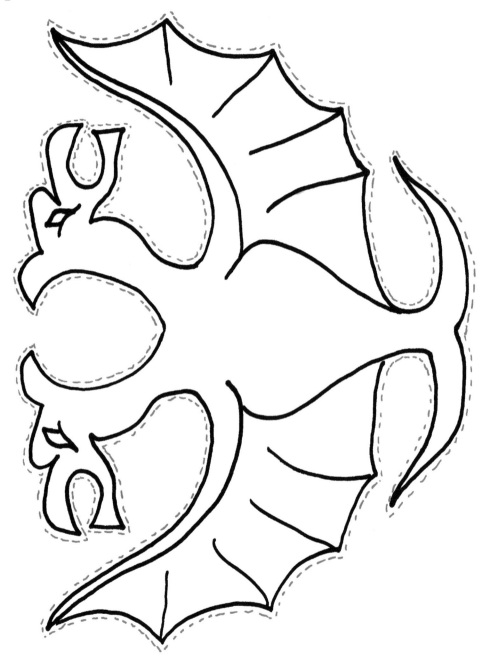

Shield Symbol

Phoenix

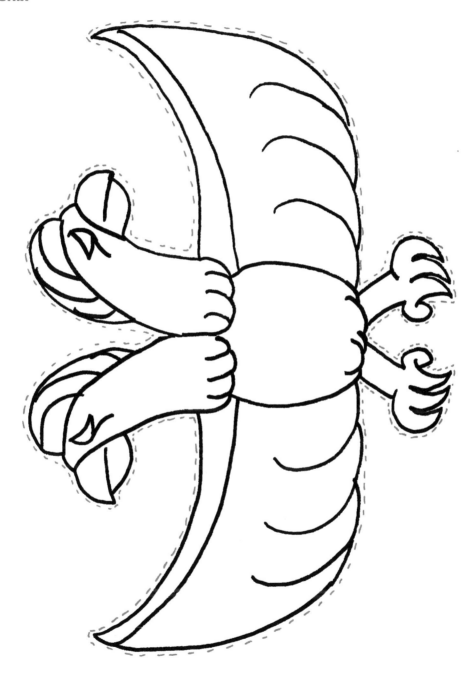

ACKNOWLEDGMENTS

Creating something out of a box is easy; getting a book published is a lot harder. That's why I have to thank, first and foremost, my agent, Kerry Sparks of Levine Greenberg, who found the right person to believe in this book, the (infinitely patient) Lara Asher of Globe Pequot Press. Thank you so much, ladies!

I also have to thank the following: author, journalist, and neighbor, Ron Lieber, who always knew this should be a book; his daughter, Kantor Lieber, who was the inspiration for our pirate journey; young Miss Ginger ("Gingy") Semmelhack, who brought boxes for our castle; the talented actor, Mr. Jeremy Kreuzer, for his magic and puppeteering skills; actress and author, Sonia Manzano, for her wonderful foreword from a box's point of view; actor and musician, Emilio Delgado (aka *Sesame Street*'s "Luis") for his wonderful words; and my fellow puppeteer/Muppeteer and friend, Peter Linz, who took the time to share a childhood memory.

Finally, I need to thank the three people who mean the most to me, for their continued faith in my ideas: my mom, Edna MacNeal ("Don't get a job; get a career"); my son, Mattie, who believes I can make *anything* out of cardboard (and so far, I have); and, most important, my wife, author of the Maggie Hope Mysteries, Susan Elia MacNeal, whose love and support keep me creating and imagining the impossible.

ABOUT THE AUTHOR

Noel MacNeal launched his career performing on PBS's award-winning *Sesame Street,* where he honed his craft alongside puppetry legends Jim Henson and Frank Oz. He's been a performer on *Sesame Street* for more than twenty years, most recently training puppeteers for *Sesame Street* co-productions in Japan, Mexico, South Africa, Palestine, Jordan, and India. He is often a regular performer with the classic Muppets.

Noel has been the spirit and voice of Bear, the gentle and lovable star of the Emmy Award–winning Disney series, *Bear in the Big Blue House,* and the Disney Channel morning series, *Breakfast with Bear.* In 2003, Noel's performance as Bear earned him a Daytime Emmy nomination as Outstanding Performer in a Children's Series. His repertoire of characters also includes Lionel on PBS's Emmy Award–winning *Between the Lions;* Kako on the Nick Jr. series, *Oobi;* and Blue on *Blue's Room.* He has also played Magellan on the Ace Award–winning series, *Eureeka's Castle,* on Nick Jr. He played Madame Chairbird in the film, *Sesame Street Presents: Follow That Bird;* Rabbit, for Disney Channel's Emmy Award–winning series, *The Book of Pooh;* Leon, on PBS's *The Puzzle Place;* and Knock-Knock, on *The Great Space Coaster.* In addition, he's performed with and/or for Woody Allen, Bill Cosby, Whoopi Goldberg, Jerry Lewis, Mickey Rooney, Emma Thompson, Wayne Brady, Dave Chappelle, Donny and Marie Osmond, Gilbert Gottfried, Tom Bergeron, Regis Philbin and Kelly Ripa, and Matt Lauer and Katie Couric. (But not all at once.)

Noel is also a television writer. His scripts have been featured on PBS Kids Sprout's *The Good Night Show,* PBS's *Cyberchase,* Disney Channel's *Bear in the Big Blue House,* PBS's *The Puzzle Place* and *The Magic Schoolbus,* Nickelodeon's *Eureeka's Castle,* and *Gullah Gullah Island.* And now he's added the credit of television director, having directed episodes of *Bear in the Big Blue House* and PBS Kids Sprout's *The Good Night Show,* and on-camera talent, as the human host of *A Very Special Good Night Show* for PBS Kids Sprout.

Noel is the author of *10-Minute Puppets,* and lives in Brooklyn, New York, with his wife, Susan, and eight-year-old son, Matthew.